HOLLYWOOD'S

LATIN
Lovers

HOLLYWOOD'S
LATIN
Lovers

LATINO, ITALIAN AND FRENCH MEN
WHO MAKE THE SCREEN SMOLDER

VICTORIA THOMAS

ANGEL CITY PRESS

ANGEL CITY PRESS, INC.
2118 Wilshire Boulevard, Suite 880
Santa Monica, California 90403
(310) 395-9982
http://www.angelcitypress.com

First published in 1998 by Angel City Press
1 3 5 7 9 10 8 6 4 2
FIRST EDITION

ISBN 1-883318-41-6

Text copyright © 1998 by Victoria Thomas

Art direction and design by Sheryl Winter

Distributed by Universe Publishing through St. Martin's Press,
175 Fifth Avenue, New York, New York 10010

Printed in Hong Kong

LIBRARY OF CONGRESS CATALOGING-IN-PUBLICATION DATA
Thomas,Victoria, 1956-
  Hollywood's Latin Lovers : Latino, French, and Italian men who
make the screen smolder / by Victoria Thomas. — 1st ed.
    p. cm.
ISBN 1-883318-41-6 (cloth)
  1. Latin lovers in motion pictures—United States.   1. Title.
PN1995.9.L38T56 1998
791.43'652034—dc21   97-45430
                                                       CIP

For my husband, Andy

TABLE OF

CONTENTS

INTRODUCTION
from stereotype to
ARCHETYPE

Hollywood's Latin Lover was the man your mother warned you about. He was the man women yearned to touch. He was the man other men yearned to become. Cinema portrayed the Latin Lover as a dark-eyed, dark-haired she-magnet, utterly at ease in his abundant, freewheeling masculinity. Although often portrayed as a bandit or tough guy, he posed his greatest danger through pure charm. He was gallant enough (when it suited him) to make even the most proper ladies swoon. And he was just caddish enough to make tamer, more domesticated men cheer him on.

Something of the warm, southern latitudes in his full lips and dark, direct gaze—his ethnic origins ranged from Paris to Paraguay—made America's heart skip a beat, from the early silents to the present day. We surrendered at once, and we are still in his power. He truly is a creature of mythology, and his enduring effect upon

No one strikes a pose like Hollywood's Latin Lover as demonstrated by Gilbert Roland, opposite, Rudolph Valentino, left, in The Four Horsemen of the Apocalypse, *(1921) and Ramon Novarro (with Greta Garbo in* Mata Hari, *1931).*

us, in spite of his political incorrectness, inspired this book.

As sheik, swashbuckler, bullfighter or mambo king, the Latin Lover was Hollywood's steamiest male persona for decades. While blond, blue-eyed actors were more consistently cast in leading roles, the Latin Lover invariably stole the show. His instant popularity with audiences, beginning with Rudolph Valentino, Antonio Moreno and Ramon Novarro, inspired Hollywood moguls to package any actor with remotely ethnic features as "Latin." Tight pants, riding boots and extravagantly rolled "R"s took him from the realm of the everyday into pure fantasy.

The Latin Lover is a *mestizo* (a mix or blend) of the imagination. He is a very powerful synthesis of ideas, initially concocted for profit by the movie studios, then nourished by the sighing human need for a dream-lover. On a superficial level, he is a dark, forbidden fruit for women. The Latin Lover appealed to men as well, because he represented their most ungentlemanly urges, unbound. His on-screen character was frequently more overtly sexual and more violent than his mainstream counterpart, thus offering vicarious liberation to female and male audiences alike.

Born as a fantasy of commerce, the Latin Lover quickly bloomed into a creature of the erotic imagination. Even before movies could talk, shrewd non-Latin film studio executives recognized the potential profit in tantalizing American women with a bit of exotic flesh, and captivated the newly created moviegoing public. So successful were these stars that their images became bankable, worthy of cloning; during the 1920s, every studio had at least one bare-chested sheik on the screen. Many Latin leading men expressed varying degrees

The Latin Lover was man enough to wear lace, and to wear it well. From the sleek Fernando Lamas, above left in Sangaree *(1953) with Arlene Dahl, to the rugged Anthony Quinn in an uncharacteristically frilly role, the Latin Lover did some of his best work in period costume.*

of exasperation with the stereotype of the guitar-strumming, cape-twirling Romeo. But in some cases, the Latin Lover role served as a gateway to more complex and contemporary roles. And for a public desperate for distraction, the Latin Lover provided a precious commodity: the fantasy of perfect, delicious maleness that makes the heart race and the knees buckle.

This book celebrates the mystique of actors of Latin descent who have burned themselves indelibly into the moviegoing consciousness. Their work represents a broad range of portrayals of a character which has become a uniquely American icon, beginning with Valentino and extending into the careers of present-day actors. Their appeal ranges from the most impeccably dapper (Fernando Lamas) to the lyrical (Charles Boyer) to the most robustly, ruggedly potent (Anthony Quinn), to an almost genderless irresistibility (Antonio Banderas).

Despite what now seem like derogatory portrayals, Hollywood had a taste for exoticism in the twenties, thirties and forties. Glamorized foreign locations, especially those evoking the click of castanets or the rustle of rumba ruffles, were box-office gold, compelling many non-Latin actors to assume Latin names, even if the characters they portrayed were of unspecified ethnicity. For instance, Jacob Krantz became "Ricardo Cortez" for roles which included Sam Spade in *The Maltese Falcon* (1931).

In the Golden Age of Hollywood, and until quite recently, the term "Latin" was applied carelessly. As often as not, non-Latins were cast in Latin roles, generally involving the stereotypical ethnic bravura. These actors, too, became classed as "Latin Lovers" by studio marketing

Jacob Krantz, above right, reinvented himself as "Ricardo Cortez" to jump on the cinematic bandwagon filled with Latin Lovers. Self-described "Latin from Manhattan" Cesar Romero starred with the smartly turned-out Carole Lombard in Love Before Breakfast *(1936).*

executives. As an example, Douglas Fairbanks, starred as *Don Q Son of Zorro* (1925) and *The Gaucho* (1927), undeterred by his true Hungarian-Jewish heritage. In the same vein, non-Latin Tyrone Power established himself as the ultra-swashbuckler in *The Mark of Zorro* (1940) and *Blood and Sand* (1941), a remake of the 1922 Valentino original.

With equal abandon, actors of Latin descent were frequently cast as Asians, Arabs, Native Americans and Greeks (and, in the case of Mexican-born Oscar-winner Anthony Quinn, all of these!). The sad truth is that Hollywood knew little about Latin cultures, histories or traditions. Latin characters were conceived and scripted with only a tourist's postcard-understanding of *Latinismo*; the results are as laughable as a souvenir sombrero (or simply insulting, depending upon your point of view). In addition to seducers, most Latin leading men have played rollicking gypsy-boys, mustachioed banditos, gangsters and other all-purpose scoundrels, roles which reinforced the notion of ethnic people as morally inferior. In this sense, Hollywood's Latin Lover was truly a man without a country.

Being cast as "ethnic" was severely limiting to an actor's career, especially since the ethnic roles which Hollywood offered were generally laced with racially and culturally-based insensitivities ranging from the merely ludicrous to the intolerably offensive. Often, a Latin actor's choices narrowed down to just two: either play a cartoon Latin, or don't play at all. Perhaps this dilemma persuaded some Latin actors, such as the son of a Juarez toreador born Luis Antonio Damaso de Alonso, to adopt Anglo-sounding names (in this case, Gilbert Roland) in an attempt to strike a manageable balance between Latin and mainstream American realities.

Non-Latin Tyrone Power was cast in the lead of the Valentino vehicle, Blood and Sand *(1941), which also featured Anthony Quinn. Quinn was often cast as a hoodlum, occasionally showing his sweet side as here with Anna Magnani in* Wild Is the Wind *(1957).*

The disparaging and insensitive term "greaser," in reference to Latins, frequently appeared in film titles. During the 1940s, the depiction of Latins, especially Mexicans, in Hollywood films was so inflammatory that the governments of the United States and Mexico intervened to establish new guidelines for writers and directors.

This book uses the term "Latin" in its most catholic sense, to embrace all people of Latin heritage (Hispanic, Latino, French, Italian and Portuguese). "Hispanic" only refers to people whose heritage traces predominantly to Spain. The term "Latino" applies to Latin people of the New World, acknowledging the African and Native American heritages of many Caribbean Latins, Mexicans, Mexican-Americans, and Central and South Americans.

Sentimentalists could argue that the tradition of the Latin Lover began with the characters whose very names are associated with moonlit balconies and throbbing loins: Romeo, Don Juan, Casanova. In fact, beginning with Rudolph Valentino, the Italian actor who whipped the nation into a frenzy with his portrayal of a long-lashed prince of Araby, Hollywood displayed a spectrum of ambivalence toward Latin actors, as well as the portrayal of Latin (and all visibly ethnic) roles.

It is a stretch to claim that the Latin Lover has firm roots as a character in any Latin literary tradition, although romantic art and literature as we define it today did, in fact, emerge from the northernmost edge of the Latin world, with the French troubadours five centuries ago. Troubadours traveled the villages of

Gilbert Roland, above with would-be star Aurelia Fairfax, began his career in the slick-haired Valentino mode, later toughening into the most credible player of The Cisco Kid. Valentino, even at his most virile, always remained the hothouse flower.

southern Europe, singing songs which retold the myths of passionate and tragic love affairs. Before the troubadours, romantic love as a reason to marry, much less *un raison d'etre*, was unthinkable.

This tradition spawned the phenomenon of courtly love during the Middle Ages, a love which was by its very definition illicit, ennobled by impossibility, and utterly doomed. This Latin sense of tragedy carried over into the twentieth century, shaping the portrayal of the Latin Lover on celluloid.

In spite of his abundant and persuasive male powers, cinema's Latin Lover often loses at love. He frequently displays a weakness for non-Latin women who are drawn helplessly by his magnetism, succumb wantonly, but finally abandon him for a less controversial companion. When the woman (wistfully) leaves her Latin Lover for a more culturally acceptable mate, Hollywood reinforces the comfortable American status quo. In this sense, movies often used the Latin Lover as the fall guy in a sort of moral fable: sex, as symbolized by handsome men from hot and uncivilized places, had to be suppressed at any cost.

At first it may seem strange that the Latin Lover, a character so explicitly defined by his wooing of women, should stand alone. It is, in fact, the Latin Lover's ability to hold himself apart from women, even as he sets their hearts aflame, which elevates him to mythic status.

From the days of the Bible, *The Odyssey* and the Koran through to the present,

Ricardo Montalban, above left, and Charles Boyer, shown here with Joan Fontaine in The Constant Nymph *(1943), were classic Latin Lovers. Maurice Chevalier, is surrounded by admirers in* The Merry Widow *(1934).*

writers have discoursed upon the male need to detach from women. The Latin Lover of the imagination manages this separation with uncanny grace, blowing a gallant kiss from his limousine or his *vaquero* saddle as he rides off into the sunset. In that moment, he makes us believe that the kiss is real, meant only for us, just as we believed his urgent, whispered promises of the midnight before were meant only for us.

Politically incorrect or not, the character of the Latin Lover was, and is, a miracle worker. He makes every woman who sees him feel unspeakably desired, and impossibly desirable. He gives even the

weariest spirit, male as well as female, a glint of much-needed wickedness. Finally, the fact that Hollywood portrayed his Latinness so clumsily becomes unimportant. He is only "Latin" by coincidence. What really matters is that he is a divinely masculine being from a warmer, more pleasurable galaxy. At his best, he transcends the biases and clichés which first formed his being on-screen. It is bliss to move with him across the dance floor pulsing with tangos, *boleros* or *cumbias*, and to sink hopelessly into his dark eyes.❖

Even playing The Cisco Kid, Cesar Romero epitomized the Latin Lover as a smooth operator, while ugly-handsome Jean-Paul Belmondo brought the character into the age of disillusionment.

RUDOLPH VALENTINO

an invitation to the

SUBLIME

She arrives by limousine at the Hollywood Cemetery Mausoleum, a wraith-like figure in black. Clasping a bouquet of roses, blood-red except for a single white bud, she makes a dramatic, austere entrance, sweeping down the corridor on her way to the crypt. To her displeasure, another woman, also in black, has preceded her, placing her spray of roses at the grave. The two exchange silent glares. A third woman enters, veiled in a mourning ensemble of bridal white, then stalks off in a huff, unwilling to compete. A third Lady in Black appears, as she does every day, and leaves a few daisies in the glass containers by the crypt. The magnetism of Rudolph Valentino persists beyond the grave.

The death of Valentino at thirty-one on August 23, 1926, was the defining moment of his career, securing his sacrificial status for eternity, and inspiring occult, obsessive rever-

Pure animal magnetism brought moviegoers in droves to experience The Great Lover, Rudolph Valentino. All future Latin Lovers were measured against his mystique and mass allure.

ence for the actor in the half-century which followed. The legendary Ladies in Black still visit Valentino's crypt, although not in the dramatic numbers reported there throughout the thirties, forties and fifties.

Valentino's death, while shocking, was far from romantic. He was not gored by a charging bull, nor run through with a foe's dagger; he died from peritonitis caused by a perforated gastric ulcer. A few years later, a shrewd Hollywood publicist named Russell Birdwell hired a five-dollar-a-day extra to visit Valentino's crypt, clad all in black. Birdwell then planted newspaper stories about the mysterious figure who made her annual homage to the fallen prince of the silent screen. The papers loved the story, the readers loved the story, and the Lady in Black, as she came to be known, became an extension of Valentino's persistent mythic persona.

The actor insisted that he was not good-looking, at least not by the local standards of beauty in his native Italy. To American audiences, however, he came to personify masculine erotic power at its most dangerous and exotic. The actor's origins in the small Italian village of Castellanata prepared him for sending the smoldering glances which made him "the other man in every woman's life," as his publicity claimed, by the mid-1920s. He explained to the press that, in Italy, eligible girls were never without their chaperones, and so young Italians, who are "always in love," learned to send messages of *amore* without words. "An American may speak love with his lips," said Valentino. "The Italian must say it with his eyes."

Silence is as crucial to the allure of Rudolph Valentino as his androgynous beauty. Although he is predated by Antonio Moreno, Valentino defines the Latin Lover of the silent era. Often photographed in stoic profile, he is as stylized and timeless as an Egyptian sphinx.

Speech, of course, would have broken the spell. His very quality of mesmerizing voicelessness makes the star's presence on the screen, as heavily ornamented and robed as a high priest, seem like a ritual or dream. Just as we never heard Valentino speak, we never had to watch him endure the indignities of growing old. In this sense, he is as eternally young and supple as the gods, preserved in his audience's memory at the peak of his lithe perfection. This Italian-Gothic cocktail of youth,

He was America's romantic dramatist in The Sheik *(1921),* The Young Rajah *(1922), right, and* The Son of the Sheik *(1926), but many film historians believe that Valentino intended these as comic roles.*

sex, fame and tragedy instantly deified Valentino, and set the precedent for what has become an American tradition of stardom cut short by early death.

Born May 6, 1895 to middle-class parents, he was christened Rodolfo Alfonzo Rafaelo Pierre Filibert Guglielmi di Valentina d'Antonguolla. His ambition had been to follow in the footsteps of his cavalry captain father, who died when the boy was eleven years old. However, poor academic grades and failure to pass the rigorous physical requirements (his chest was too narrow!) at the Royal Naval Academy landed the adolescent Valentino in a local agricultural school. Were it not for the granny-knots of fate which shaped Valentino's life, the Sultan of Swoon might have spent his days quietly farming garbanzos instead of inciting outbreaks of public panic.

> **We never had to watch him endure the indignities of growing old. He is as eternally young and supple as the gods.**

After moving to America, Valentino used his knowledge of plants and gardening, and initially found work as a groundskeeper's assistant on a suburban Long Island estate. When destiny placed him in a boarding house with a Victrola, he began his career as a private dance instructor, and danced at Maxim's in New York City. He then traveled to Los Angeles and joined the short-lived touring company of a musical comedy, *The Masked Model*. For his first film appearance as a dress extra in a ballroom scene in *Alimony* (1918), he was paid five dollars for a day's work. However, the bit part, the first of seventeen minor roles to follow, was auspicious: on the set, he met another extra named Alice Taffe, who would later star with him under the stage name Alice Terry in the pivotal film of his early career, *The Four Horsemen of the Apocalypse* (1921), the same year they worked together in *The Conquering Power*. He made nine films in two years, including *Out of Luck* (a.k.a. *Nobody Home*) in 1919 with Dorothy Gish. The wheels of fate were turning.

It is fair to say that Valentino was an instant star; it just took his

Valentino, with co-star Alice Terry, became an icon after his startling death. When his fever reached one hundred five degrees, the Daily Mirror *ran the headline "Valentino Dying," and sold photos of him for five cents.*

billing a while to catch up. In the seven years before his death, after being cast in a flurry of swarthy villain roles, he went on to star in fourteen major films, most notably *Camille* (1921), *The Sheik* (1921), *Blood and Sand, The Young Rajah*, and *Beyond the Rocks* (all 1922) with Gloria Swanson, and *The Son of the Sheik* (1926). In each case he is memorable, perhaps most especially when the films themselves are not.

Valentino's skill on the dance floor again stood him in good stead as he performed a sinuous tango with Helena Domingues in *The Four Horsemen,* clad in Hollywood's rather fanciful interpretation of Argentine gaucho garb. But authenticity be damned: America got a taste, and wanted more. Wags throughout the ages have said that dancing is a vertical expression of a horizontal intention, and this was never more true than in the sensuous moves of Valentino. In addition to establishing the actor's irresistible sexual allure, the film also reoriented his screen persona from greaser-thug to a dancer with a hero's heart: his character, Julio Desnoyers, gives his life in World War I. Non-Latin leading men were seemingly directed to handle women awkwardly on camera, their clumsiness and clunkiness somehow confirming their virtue. Valentino's character, by contrast, was unflappable when approaching women on-screen. As Julio, he introduced moviegoers to a new genre, that of the noble seducer. Before Metro Studios had the savvy to capitalize upon the escalating Valentino phenomenon, Paramount signed him to play The Sheik.

The critics were unimpressed. According to the *New York Times*, November 11, 1921, "The acting could not be worse than the story, but it is bad enough. Mr. Valentino is revealed as a player without resource. He depicts the fundamental emotions of the Arabian sheik chiefly by showing his teeth and rolling his eyes." However, the public felt otherwise. By 1924, the film had earned one million dollars; even fourteen years later in 1938, well after the advent of sound, the film enjoyed a successful revival tour when it was reissued with a music track.

The artifice of the era suited Valentino far more so than it did other actors of the time, magnifying an ambiguously feminine undercurrent in his screen presence. This ambiguity is the essence of his continuing popularity; unlike klutzy, All-American leading men, this shadow-faun promised a woman (or a man) unspeakable pleasures with his eyes.

Although his costume roles may have seemed laughable to critics from the beginning, his absolute detachment from pedestrian experience fixed him in the realm of the mythic.

Valentino's personal life was far from pedestrian, characterized instead by disastrous unions with strong-willed women. He met a successful actress named Jean Acker at a party, and they were married soon after, perhaps as a marriage of convenience, at a friend's bon voyage party. Bon voyage, indeed; the marriage lasted six hours, according to some sources because Acker was a lesbian. In 1921, during the making of *Camille*, he met set and costume designer Natacha Rambova (another change-

Falling for Valentino was like having a reckless affair while on vacation. The distance from home and "real" life made wild abandon seem like reasonable behavior. Above, with Nita Naldi in Cobra *(1925), he strikes the classic passion pose; above right, the classic fashion pose.*

ling, she was actually born Winifred Shaughnessy in Salt Lake City). Aesthetically, their match seemed fated. They married in Mexicali, and on May 20, 1922, Valentino surrendered to the Los Angeles police department on charges of bigamy; his divorce from Acker was not yet finalized.

Rambova took on an invasive role as Valentino's production supervisor, and her creative instincts were less than commercial. She was eventually barred from the sets of his films, so he left Paramount in 1923 to pursue independent production with her. The following year, at her insistence, Valentino starred in *Monsieur Beaucaire,* the film which prompted the *Chicago Tribune* to call him a "painted pansy" and a "pink powder puff," as well as a poor example to American boys. Dandied up in powdered wig and beauty mark, Valentino had crossed the threshold of public tolerance; he was now perceived as undeniably weak and effeminate (wearing a slave bracelet that Rambova gave him didn't help matters). When he challenged the writer of the *Tribune* editorial to a duel, he only invoked more derision.

> . . . his absolute detachment from pedestrian experience fixed him firmly in the realm of the mythic.

Valentino began a much-publicized affair with Paramount goldmine Pola Negri, arch-rival of Gloria Swanson and star of *Forbidden Paradise* (1924). Negri was perhaps the most high-visibility of the mourners at Valentino's funeral, strategically revealing to reporters that, although never formally engaged, she and Valentino had planned to marry the following spring. To say the least, she was outnumbered. The funeral coach which transported the body from New York to Los Angeles was thronged by thousands of keening female fans at every whistle stop, and on the day of his funeral, over one hundred thousand women took to the streets in a display of public grief as extravagant as the acting of The Sheik himself.

Valentino's silken sexuality is charged with the additional, electric thrill of his youthful death. He cast himself in the roles of both

Persephone and Lord Hades, pulled down from the sunlit meadow for his long season in the underworld. And year after year, he is Osiris, traveling from the land of the dead to renew his bond with those of us who remain behind. Watching his films, many still sit rapt, in mute darkness, and await his return. ❖

Valentino's chemistry with Alice Terry, opposite in The Conquering Power *(1921), was suffused with the feminine aspect of his own character. Valentino's androgynous appearance in* Monsieur Beaucaire *(1924) struck the media as suspect, yet the public clamored for more.*

RAMON NOVARRO
against the
CURRENT

He played the title role in the most expensive silent film ever made, but audiences were more interested in his bared chest as charioteer Ben-Hur than in the five-million-dollar budget. The makers of *The Pagan* (1929) strategically included his clear tenor singing the romantic title theme, "Pagan Love Song," to make the film more competitive with those newfangled talkies, but it was the star's skimpy sarong, not sound, which caused the epidemic of front-row fainting. MGM sent out hundreds of thousands of Valentines each year to the admirers who wrote him fervid fan-letters. Eminent director Rex Ingram described him as having " . . . the physique of Michelangelo's David and the face of an El Greco Don." But he was not what he appeared.

The advent of sound ended the careers of many silent stars, but Ramon Novarro made a strong comeback in the early talkie Mata Hari *(1931) with Greta Garbo.*

He was the most truly beautiful of the silent era Latin Lovers, and a more gifted actor by far than his friend Rudolph Valentino, yet he was quick to brush off any rumors of romance, which were curiously few. The studios explained that the actor, dubbed "Ravishing Ramon" by his publicists, eschewed the fast living of many of his peers because of his strong religious beliefs, and had often considered joining a monastic order. He never married, dismissing matrimony as "one mistake I did not make." His refusal to tie the knot was the undoing of his career. The reasons for his refusal proved to be the undoing of the man.

In 1921, five years before he starred as the lissome, nearly-naked Ben-Hur in the silent classic by the same name, Ramon Novarro, then known as Ramon Samaniegos, played a bit part in Rex Ingram's *The Four Horsemen of the Apocalypse* (1921) with Valentino. When Valentino left Metro for Paramount because the studio refused him a fifty-dollar-a-week raise, a vacuum was created at Metro, since sloe-eyed lover-types who looked good in turbans were cinema's hottest ticket.

At Ingram's suggestion, Samaniegos adopted one of his fourteen baptismal names, a surname from his mother's side of the family, and became Ramon Novarro for his next role in *Trifling Women* (1922). Samuel Goldwyn saw the picture before it was released, and offered Novarro a two-

The star's skimpy sarong, not sound, caused the epidemic of front-row fainting.

year contract at two thousand dollars a week, an offer Novarro spurned out of loyalty to Ingram. Novarro also resented the fact that Goldwyn had turned down his earlier screen test. More importantly, Goldwyn had committed a cardinal sin, having secretly gone to Novarro's family to enlist their support in swaying the actor's opinion. Novarro guarded his private life fiercely. Such intrusions were the reason for his reclusive withdrawal from Hollywood.

The fourth picture of the Ingram-Novarro collaboration, *Where the Pavement Ends* (1923), cast Novarro opposite Alice Terry, who became Ingram's wife. The film's South Seas plot, as scanty as Novarro's wardrobe, typified Hollywood's view of ethnic actors. Novarro and Terry

Novarro's screen debut was as a turbaned dancer in a slapstick harem scene in A Small Town Idol *(1921). Opposite, he's a turbaned sheik again in* The Barbarian *(1933) with Myrna Loy.*

play a smooth-skinned jungle boy and a repressed white missionary's daughter who share a taboo attraction (The drums! The drums!). In the original cut, a despairing Novarro drowns himself in a waterfall at the end of the film. Shortly after its release, however, as Novarro's devoted fans grew ever-zealous, movie exhibitors demanded a new, feel-good ending. Ingram recalled all the prints, and re-released the film which climaxes with the discovery that Novarro's parents were Caucasian after all.

Scaramouche (1923) again featured Novarro with Lewis Stone and Alice Terry, this time against the romance of the French Revolution. *The Arab* (1924), which would be Ingram's final Hollywood endeavor, played out his foolproof formula one last time—picture-postcard foreign setting, Terry and Novarro trapped in a forbidden passion. "Ramon Novarro is one hundred and ten degrees in the shade!" panted the advertisements for the film, and much-publicized bodyguards manned the set to detain any overly amorous *aficionadas* who had the wherewithal to sail to the North African location. Novarro starred in the MGM talkie remake as well, *The Barbarian* (1933).

Novarro returned to California and made two films directed by Fred Niblo: *Thy Name is Woman* (1924) and *The Red Lily* (1924). Then came the offer from MGM: a guaranteed ten thousand dollars a week. Even without Ingram, Novarro's career was beginning a dazzling, if brief, climb.

Born Jose Ramon Gil Samaniegos on February 6, 1899 in Durango, Mexico, Ramon was the eldest of thirteen children. When he and one of his brothers were invited to visit relatives in El Paso, Texas, the

In The Pagan *(1929) with Dorothy Janis, the Latin Lover traded his turban for a sarong. "Ravishing Ramon" had a tropical effect upon moviegoers.*

two boys almost immediately headed for California, with only ten dollars between them.

Unwilling to abandon his dream of performing, but anxious to provide support for his mother and siblings, Ramon took odd jobs as a grocery clerk, theater usher, piano teacher, cafe singer and busboy at the elegant Alexandria Hotel. By the late teens, the swank hotel bar had become a gathering-spot for aspiring actors, and it was there that Novarro first met Valentino, who was then a featured dancer.

Novarro was a gifted dancer and singer as well, and had worked briefly in vaudeville in New York City with Marion Morgan's touring company. Back in Hollywood, both Ramon and his oldest sister Carmen easily found work as studio dance extras. Ramon appeared in several different Vitagraph serials and Ince productions, including *The Little American* (1917) starring Mary Pickford, directed by Cecil B. De Mille, *The Jaguar's Claws* (1917), *The Hostage* (1917), De Mille's *Joan the Woman* (1917), *The Goat* (1918), and others.

In 1921, he appeared in a Mack Sennett comedy, *A Small Town Idol*, and was cast that same year by Rex Ingram in *The Four Horsemen of the Apocalypse*. Ingram had seen Novarro perform a dance pantomime, "The Royal Fandango," at the Hollywood Community Theater, and director Ferdinand Pinney Earle had shown him a few of Novarro's scenes from his art film, *The Rubaiyat of Omar Khayyam* (released in 1925 as *A Lover's Oath*) before the actor approached him about his next role as the wonderfully wicked Rupert von Hentzau in *The Prisoner of Zenda* (1922).

The pseudo-literary content of the story was a satisfactory smoke-

Just as Valentino oozed reptilian worldliness and knowing, Novarro maintained an aura of youthful innocence. He was heroic as Ben-Hur, left, and boyish with Jeanette MacDonald in The Cat and the Fiddle *(1934).*

screen for the basic prurience of the film, which relied heavily upon Novarro's exposed, taut limbs and the titillating mix of bare skin, charging stallions, sweat, bondage and violence. Valentino's sudden death in August of the same year made Novarro the reigning Latin Lover of American cinema. He filled the role well.

After *Ben-Hur*, Novarro made several films back to back, and by now

he led the life of a star, tooling around town in a sleek 1928 Lincoln roadster and holding court in his sprawling seventeen-room estate in the West Adams district. Built to his specifications to accommodate a private theater, *El Teatro Intimo*, noted performers entertained there at his invitation, and Novarro himself often sang to the star-studded audiences he gathered. The actor was considering an alternate career in opera.

After making *The Student Prince* (1927) with Norma Shearer, Novarro began to pull away from the limelight which had adoringly bathed his Adonis-like being. He claimed that he was bored, and admitted to the press that he resented the violations of his privacy which stardom seemed to require. He even stopped singing in the choir of the Church of Our Lady of Guadalupe, he said, because he was being pestered by autograph-seekers. Privacy was increasingly precious to Novarro because he had a secret to protect: Ravishing Ramon preferred the intimate pleasures of other beautiful males, a predilection which could turn even the most golden career into box office poison. And as the stakes grew higher, so did the risk of discovery.

Perhaps because Novarro was in subtle retreat from his own fame, the star's public identity was beginning to wane. In addition, the classic Latin Lover roles were being replaced by tough-guy gangster characters; times had changed, and the moony exotica of the twenties had been replaced by the grit of the Great Depression. MGM's Irving Thalberg desperately cast him in a motley array of incongruous roles, ranging from Asians and Native Americans to a Caucasian football hero.

Then, in 1932, Novarro regained his stellar footing opposite Greta Garbo in *Mata Hari*. The two stars wrote their own fabulously kitschy love scene which suggests their stylized embrace with the firefly-like path of their burning cigarette-tips in total darkness. The studios eagerly fed rumors of romance between the stars, which Novarro instantly and flatly quashed. Two years later, when similar gossip arose linking Novarro with Myrna Loy, he made it clear that there would never be wedding bells in his future. In 1934, he told the *Los Angeles Times*, "Women? Phooey! Marriage? Not for me. There's never been a successful marriage in Hollywood . . . I've never been in love."

Despite the star's obvious aversion to matrimony, Louis B. Mayer was intent upon finding him a mate for publicity purposes. Novarro refused, and the death-knell for his career sounded, although in interviews he named ugly contract disputes as the cause.

Virtually blackballed from Hollywood, Novarro filmed the Italian-made *La Comedie de Bonheur* (1940, the better-known Italian-dubbed version is *Ecco la Felicita*) with Louis Jourdan. As Europe prepared for World War II, the film's French director had to return to Paris, and Novarro finished directing the picture himself; unfortunately, it received very few bookings in America under either title.

He played road tours and summer stock, as well as occasional character roles in films. When his mother died in 1949, Novarro sold his estate, and built a smaller home in leafy Laurel Canyon, assuming a life of semi-solitude and near-anonymity, comforted by the fact that his siblings lived nearby. In the 1960s, he

Louis B. Mayer permitted Novarro to make only one film every two years while under contract to MGM, to prevent him from being overexposed to a fickle public. The reclusive actor said, "My idea of hell is to be a star all your life."

made rare television appearances, on "Combat" and the "Wild, Wild West."

Recurring bouts of pleurisy requiring hospitalization, immobilizing arthritis, and a series of arrests for drunk driving seemed a bittersweet adagio for the once blithe spirit of the silent screen.

On Halloween morning, 1968, police made the horrifying discovery that Novarro had been beaten to death by a young hustler and his teenage brother. The brothers had learned of Novarro through a family friend, and visited the home in search of the five thousand dollars the sixty-nine-year-old actor allegedly always kept stashed in the house. The details of the alcohol-laced murder were lurid, and much embellished by movie historians since. Novarro had not had a starring role in twenty-eight years, and it had been eight years since he had appeared in a film. But, with the caprice that is typical of Hollywood, his grisly death turned him into Page One material one last time. ❖

ANTONIO MORENO

the screen's first

SHEIK

Most people think of Rudolph Valentino and Ramon Novarro as the first Latin Lovers of the silver screen, because, in fact, they are more memorable as personalities, Valentino for his turbaned kitsch, and the young Novarro for his ethereal sweetness. However, it was Antonio Moreno, the first Spanish-speaking star in the United States, who created the framework for what was to become one of Hollywood's most lucrative—and often most ludicrous—inventions, the character of the Latin Lover.

The concept of studios and "stars" was new when Moreno began his career in 1912, and the enthused feminine response to his films set the precedent for the fevered fan culture which was cultivated around Valentino and Novarro almost a decade later. Valentino

Moreno's dark expressive face "read" better on camera than the less defined features of fair-haired actors, making him a natural for the primitive shooting conditions of the serials and early silents.

suggested a certain forcefulness, with his popped eyes and lingering, nibbling kisses. Novarro, especially in his South Seas roles, presented a heartbreaking sensuousness. Moreno projected none of the angst of these characters; instead, he was a gentleman, albeit a gentleman with melting, dark eyes and caramel skin. He was born Antonio Garrido Monteagudo y Moreno, in Madrid, probably on September 26, 1887 (reports vary wildly, complicated by the fact that Moreno was always coy about his age).

Of his only wife, oil heiress Daisy Canfield Danziger, Moreno told reporters, "Like a Spanish cavalier, I would gladly prostrate myself on the street so she could step on me. Look at her, a woman admired and adored by everyone. And what am I? Nothing but a poor motion picture actor." Moreno certainly was not poor when he married the divorced socialite on January 27, 1923, but the union surely made him richer. He was by then, at the age of thirty-five, Paramount's leading man. Paramount released three of his most successful features that same year, *The Trail of the Lonesome Pine* with Mary Miles Minter, *The Spanish Dancer* with Pola Negri, in which he was accused of imitating Douglas Fairbanks, and *My American Wife* with Gloria Swanson.

In every respect, 1923 was the apex of his life. Moreno had once seemed a confirmed bachelor, telling the press that loneliness was " . . . the only disadvantage of being a bachelor, but I'd hate to give up my independence . . . Sure, some American girls would make good wives, but most want to be put on a pedestal and looked up to." Which is, of course, precisely what Moreno did with Daisy Danziger. Her wealth alone inspired awe. The daughter of California oil tycoon Charles A. Canfield, she had divorced another oil millionaire, J.M. Danziger, one-time partner of fellow oil magnate E.L. Doheny, in 1922. The match elevated

Moreno's already-considerable status.

After his initial stage work in New York, Moreno became an almost instant institution in popular studio serials, which he gladly abandoned for feature roles once he had achieved leverage as a star draw. Introduced by his role in the 1912 one-reeler, *Voice of the Million,* Moreno began working with D.W. Griffith (and occasionally with Mack Sennett) for Biograph serials that same year. His leading ladies were the era's most beloved names, including Mary Pickford and the Gish sisters; he also starred with Lionel Barrymore in *Oil and Water* (1913) and *No Place For Father* (1913).

In 1914, Alfred E. Smith signed Moreno to the rival serial studio Vitagraph. Occasionally, as in *The Tarantula* (1916), or *The Iron Test* (1918) in which he played a circus acrobat, the serials would showcase Moreno's athletic form, but most episodes were wooden even by the period's own rather unsophisticated dramatic standards. Just as his olive complexion was hidden beneath a thick mask of theatrical makeup, Moreno believed that his talent was masked by the formulaic serial genre as well.

The cliffhangers consisted of fifteen to twenty weekly installments, in which the cast was subjected to all manner of catastrophe, both natural and man-made. The action consisted primarily of villains and stoic heroes, grappling over swooning, frequently hysterical women. Perhaps seeking less predictable material, Moreno left Vitagraph for a year and worked for Pathé studios, where he made the artistically superior *The Naulahka* (1918), a Rudyard Kipling yarn, as well as *The House of Hate* (1918), a twenty-part serial with Pearl White which was so successful that Smith was compelled to lure Moreno back to Vitagraph with a fatter contract. After three fifteen-part serials, *The Perils of Thunder Mountain* (1919), *The Invisible Hand* (1919) and *The Veiled Mystery* (1920), Moreno

After battling fires, blizzards, avalanches and floods in approximately eighty cliffhanger melodramas for Vitagraph and Pathé between 1914 and 1920, Moreno contended with another force of nature—Greta Garbo—in The Temptress *(1926).*

insisted upon being cast in star vehicles. Smith resisted, not wanting to tamper with his winning formula, and so the star broke away, made two B-pictures for Goldwyn, and then was signed by Paramount.

Riding the crest of his career at Paramount, Moreno and his bride built an estate named "Crestmont," located in the area of Los Angeles now known as Silver Lake. The twenty-one-thousand-square-foot compound with its twenty-two rooms and seventy-five-foot pool was designed by Robert Farquhar, better-known for the design of the Pentagon, and became the site for lavish Sunday parties in the golden years before Black Tuesday.

> **He was a gentleman, albeit a gentleman with melting, dark eyes and caramel skin.**

His career remained in top form through the late twenties, which paired him with both Greta Garbo in her second American film, *The Temptress* (1926), and with the scintillating Clara Bow in *It* (1927). Just as he had expertly played the serial studios against each other to his own advantage, Moreno was not above the occasional display of diva temperament on the set. When *Temptress* director Mauritz Stiller asked Moreno to wear a huge pair of shoes to make Garbo's feet appear smaller, he walked off the production; Fred Niblo, who would also direct Novarro, replaced Stiller, and the resulting film was one of the most successful of Moreno's career.

Moreno made between eighty-five and ninety silents. Then, in 1930, the major studios launched a massive re-marketing campaign to flood the European and Latin American markets with Spanish-language versions of their releases. This work alone consumed Moreno for four or five years. The *Pittsburgh Press* said in jest that Hollywood had forgotten that Moreno could speak English, but it was nearly true. Prior to being cast in *Voice of the Million* (1912), he had performed in vaudeville with Beatrice Ingraham in New York, worked as a stock star with the Manhattan Players, and appeared in *Thais* with Constance Collier and Tyrone Power, Sr., Wilton Lackaye's stage production of *The Right To Happiness,* and the musical *The Man from Cook's*, as well as several other

In 1913, Moreno appeared in one of the first full-length silents, Judith of Bethulia. *After his success in* It *(1927) with Clara Bow, he became Paramount's top leading man.*

plays. Yet, in spite of his considerable success in silents and his facility with live theater, Moreno was not successful in crossing over into English-language talkies as a featured player.

The brilliant sun of Moreno's career had turned into a waning moon. In 1931, he went to Mexico to direct the first Mexican talkie, called *Aguilas Frente El Sol* (*Eagles Before the Sun*), which earned a million pesos. He and Daisy became estranged, then separated, with Daisy taking an apartment at the Fontenoy in Los Angeles, and Moreno taking up residence at the Hollywood Athletic Club. Both parties stolidly asserted to the press that the "friendly" split would not lead to divorce. Then, in the pre-dawn fog of Mulholland Drive, February 23, 1933, the Morenos' life took a tragic turn—literally.

Forty-five-year-old Daisy, one of the West Coast's leading arbiters of taste in high society, was returning from a dance at the Beverly Wilshire Hotel. Behind the wheel was twenty-one year-old Rene Dussaq, nephew of the lifelong friend who had first sponsored Moreno when he arrived in the United States in 1902. At Daisy's insistence, they took Mulholland, perilous even in the daylight because of its sudden, hairpin turns; she had told him that the stunning mountain views were reminiscent of his native Switzerland.

Following behind Daisy's sedan were her daughter, Beth (from her marriage to Danziger) and son-in-law Francis Tappaan. The canyon passes of the Hollywood Hills are filled with mist in the winter months; visibility was particularly poor that morning, causing Dussaq to turn the knob which he thought would make the touring car's headlights brighter as they rounded a sharp turn. Instead, he turned the headlights off completely, and immediately lost his sense of the winding road in the foggy darkness. The car plunged three hundred feet over the embankment, rolling over several times and crushing Daisy in the fall. Miraculously, Dussaq was able to drag himself up the hillside to the road, in spite of a broken vertebra and internal injuries, and flagged down a

Moreno was Hollywood's most eligible bachelor until he was thirty-five. His famous couplings were limited to his screen pairings with the likes of Mary Pickford, Lillian and Dorothy Gish, Greta Garbo and Irene Castle.

passing motorist. At the time of her death, Daisy's assets were estimated in excess of one million dollars.

Moreno's roles in the later thirties—*The Bohemian Girl* (1936), *Rose of the Rio Grande* (1938)—were scarce, and did not resuscitate his career. In 1947, he appeared as Tyrone Power's father in *Captain from Castile*, followed by *Crisis* (1950) with peers Gilbert Roland and Ramon Novarro.

Moreno forfeited much of his wealth in an unsuccessful real estate venture called Moreno Highlands as Crestmont, once a rival of Pickfair, began a series of new incarnations. In 1953, the estate was turned over to the Franciscan Missionary Sisters of the Immaculate Conception, and was transformed into Our Lady of the Sacred Heart girls' home.

Late in his life, Moreno played character roles, including *The Searchers* (1950) directed by John Ford, and his last picture, *Dallas* (1950), starring Gary Cooper. His death in 1967 brought down the curtain on an era, as well as one of its earliest, brightest stars. ❖

Moreno made many bilingual films and directed films in Mexico including Aguilas Frente al Sol *(1931). After the introduction of sound, Moreno appeared in westerns but he was at his best in suave, silent roles.*

GILBERT ROLAND

and the crowd roars

"¡OLE!"

In December, 1995, a pair of ladies' underpants—circa 1943, with "G.G." mono-grammed on cream-colored silk—were appraised at one hundred fifty thousand dollars by Christie's auction house in New York. Also part of the package was a military knapsack that belonged to Gilbert Roland, a two-year veteran of World War II. The panties were Greta Garbo's. How these two items came to be sold together after fifty years is to under-stand the staying power of Gilbert Roland.

News of the affair between the two silver screen giants surprised even movie histori-ans; Garbo had never mentioned Roland. In 1943 he was thirty-eight years old, married to his one-time co-star Constance Bennett, and no longer the box-office draw he had been.

Luis Antonio Damasco de Alonso, son of a Juarez toreador, changed his name to Gilbert Roland, replacing the pensive sensitivity of earlier Latin Lovers with pistola-slinging virility.

Garbo had retired from film two years earlier. While on leave in Los Angeles, he stopped at his Beverly Hills tailor and noticed a pair of ladies' trousers intended for Garbo. Roland delivered the garment to her home; she appeared a few hours later at his door, and spent the night.

They parted the next morning. Roland tucked the panties into his coat pocket as he boarded the army transport plane back to the field, and carried them in his knapsack for the next two years, along with thirteen love letters from Garbo, in which she refers to him as her "little soldier boy" and "the mountain boy." Of course, Roland also packed along *billet-doux* from Norma Talmadge and Clara Bow, his co-stars who had both called him "the great love of my life." What is most telling about Roland as a man is not that he bedded the inscrutable Garbo, but rather that the world never knew. For an *hombre* literally born to the arena, Roland was astonishingly discreet.

Even in his more public affairs, Roland never played the kiss-and-tell cad. When his long-time love and co-star Norma Talmadge married another man, Louella Parsons wrote, "the torch Gilbert carried lighted up the whole town." True, he preened, strutted, always sported a debonair moustache, enjoyed a good bullfight and a good glass of red Spanish wine. An unapologetic clotheshorse, fond of flashy clothes which flaunted his famous twenty-nine-inch waist, Roland wore his stylish whites and knotted cashmere sweaters at the Beverly Hills Tennis Club the way a matador wore his suit of lights. Yet for all his dash he was not uncouth, never a man to let it all hang out boorishly.

> **Roland wore his stylish tennis whites the way a matador wore his suit of lights.**

Of course, he carried a picture of a woman. But it wasn't the image of his longtime flame Doris Duke, "the richest girl in the world," or one of his earlier ladies-in-waiting (Bebe Daniels, Viola Dana, Barbara La Marr, Blanche Sweet, Billie Dove). Instead, Roland cherished a small photograph of a gray-haired schoolteacher, Alma Bartlett, who had taught him to speak English in El Paso; he wrote to her throughout his career, and visited her nearly every holiday season. And the gold ring on his hand was not inscribed with a fervid endearment from a lover: the ring bore his mother's dying words *en español* ("Son, don't hurry, don't worry, good-bye, my soul").

He embodied the athletic yet mannerly swashbuckler, and his stamina and refusal to age permitted him to resurrect his faltering career more than once, most dramatically in John Huston's *We Were Strangers* (1949), and again in *The Bullfighter and the Lady* (1951).

Born in 1905 as Luis Antonio Damaso de Alonso in Ciudad Juarez in the Mexican state of Chihuahua, he was a fourth generation bullfighter. Luis practiced his own skills as a *torero* with the family goats, and worked in the Juarez bullring owned by his father, Francisco "Paquiro" Alonso, sharpening swords, selling cushions and distributing programs, for which he was paid a single peso.

When Pancho Villa attacked Ciudad Juarez, the prosperous Alonso family and other Spanish emigrants fled across the border into Texas, where Luis saw his first motion picture. By the sixth grade, as he recalled in his memoirs, "I was the biggest movie fan in the world," playing hookey from school to watch serials at a local movie house. At night by the light of a kerosene lamp, the boy would write to his favorite stars, asking for their photographs. He continued to collect stars' photos as an adult, as well as priceless photos of the world's great matadors.

In his teens, Roland hopped a freight train bound for Hollywood. Photogenic and courtly, he easily got work as an extra, finding himself in the company of stars such as Clark Gable, Charlie Farrell and Gary Cooper. Combining the names of his two favorite stars, Jack Gilbert and Ruth Roland, he quickly rechristened himself with a new, All-American identity. Preceded by his family's reputation in bullfighting, he was permitted to help dress Valentino for his role as a bullfighter in *Blood and Sand* (1922). He also doubled for Ramon Novarro in

Roland was at his rough-hewn best with Barbara Stanwyck in The Furies *(1950), Their characters scandalized a small town with their cross-cultural love affair.*

The Midshipman (1925) for seventy-five dollars a week, where he was tossed into the icy waters of the Chesapeake Bay at two in the morning for a crucial scene.

Then Roland was spotted by the "It" Girl herself, Clara Bow, who selected him to star with her in a campus comedy, *The Plastic Age* (1925). He played the male lead of Armand Duval in the silent version of Alexandre Dumas' immortal *Camille* (1927) opposite Norma Talmadge (igniting a long affair), a role he would recreate in 1933 on stage with Jane Cowl. By his early twenties, Roland had embarked upon a career that would span nearly sixty years and more than one hundred films.

When Roland's romance with Talmadge ended and she left the screen, his own star dimmed. During the 1930s, he appeared almost exclusively in B-pictures, rarely attracting roles in high-quality films. By the Great Depression, Hollywood's focus had turned to lavish, escapist musicals, a genre unsuited to Roland's interests or his talents.

In those years, his personal life was equally unsettling. In 1933, the year they starred together in *Our Betters* and *After Tonight,* he and Constance Bennett first caught the attention of gossip columnists. The couple denied any entanglement for eight years. At last confirming the gossip, they married in 1941. But after having two daughters, Lorinda and Gyl, the Rolands divorced three years later.

He then found a new audience as the dashing Mexican version of Robin Hood in six *Cisco Kid* movies in 1946 and 1947. Of the roles that he might have perceived as a big step down from Dumas' Duval, he com-

In Camille *(1933) with Norma Talmadge, opposite, Roland took an unsentimental approach to women on-screen. The same tack suited Mae West's hard-boiled heroine in* She Done Him Wrong *(1933), above, just fine.*

mented, "My Cisco Kid might have been a bandit, but he fought for the poor and was a civilized man in the true sense of the word." Roland fought the industry's tendency to stereotype Mexicans and Mexican-Americans as "*payasos*" (clowns), and insisted on frequent script changes to alter this depiction.

In one memorable instance, Roland insisted that a scene be written with The Cisco Kid reading Shakespeare on a riverbank because, "I wanted to be sure the *mexicano* was not portrayed as an unwashed, un-educated, savage clown." His own attachment to Mexico lasted all of his life; he was fond of driving across the border with a car-load of toys and dolls, and handing them out to every child he met.

Then, in 1951, making *The Bullfighter and the Lady* with Robert Stack and Joy Page brought Roland full circle. Flanked by working mata-

dors in the pageant of finery and gore, he was as taut as an arrow, art mirroring life. After all, he had been on the brink of traveling to Spain to train as a bullfighter just before he got his first call for extra-work so many years earlier. He had come full circle.

By the mid-fifties, life was good again for Roland. He was back in the movies and his romantic life was at a high point. Discreet to the point of being secretive, he married Guillermina Cantu, a twenty-nine-year-old native of Mexico City, and the marriage was not revealed until a month after the fact, in January, 1955.

His curls stayed as blue-black as Superman's, in spite of his advancing years.

The next decade yielded several successful films, including *Cheyenne Autumn* (1964) with Dolores Del Rio, *Beneath the Twelve-Mile Reef* (1953) which Roland described as having "*cojones,*" *My Six Convicts, The Miracle of Our Lady of Fatima* and *The Bad and the Beautiful* (all 1952).

Roland's gallant nature again made headlines in 1964, during the making of *The Reward* in the Arizona desert. During the shoot, he invited director Serge Bourbignon and co-star Max von Sydow to join him for their first *corrida* nearby in the town of Nogales. The scheduled bullfighter was a woman, a young Canadian named Carolyn Hayward. Roland visited her before she entered the ring, leaving her with a hug and the customary bullfighter's parting words, *hasta luego* ("See you later"). Roland took his seat in the front row and she dedicated the first bull to him. Within minutes, however, the bull had hooked Hayward and tossed her to the ground, where she lay inert. As the animal charged a second time, Roland dropped the ten feet from his seat into the ring and

Gilbert Roland was always alongside Hollywood's most voluptuous vixens, but his high-test machismo met its lusty match in that full-figured gal, Jane Russell, in The French Line *(1954).*

carried Hayward to safety.

He continued to work throughout the 1970s. His curls stayed as blue-black as Superman's, in spite of his advancing years. A black leather wrist brace, prescribed by a doctor years earlier for a tennis injury to his forearm, became his trademark, preserving his active, manly image. When prostate cancer took his life at his Beverly Hills home in 1994 at the age of eighty-eight, Roland's public grieved for the *caballero* who was too kind to be truly cavalier, and his colleagues mourned the man they knew best by his nickname: *Amigo.*❖

Roland achieved a balance between naturalness and cock-of-the-walk vanity. The bandito stereotype dogged Latin actors, but Roland portrayed Cisco as an intellectual character who happened to be the fastest gun in the West.

CESAR ROMERO

the gay CABALLERO

Acting might be considered a form of lying, and if so, Cesar Romero was a great liar. Impossibly debonair until the end of his long life, he lied to us all the time, and his lies were as polished as a string of pearls. For four decades, he positively charmed us into going along for the ride, against our better judgement. Ludicrous scripts that might have turned into leaden cream puffs in the hands of most other actors sparkled when Romero was on-screen. His eyes sparkled, too, with just enough self-mocking. Come on, he seemed to be saying, you and I both know this is absurd. But let's dance anyway.

Romero literally danced his way into motion pictures, and jumbo musicals like *Weekend in Havana* (1941), *Coney Island* (1943), *Carnival in Costa Rica (1947), Springtime in*

In the world before the anti-hero, immaculately coiffed Latin Lovers like Cesar Romero ruled the screen. The title of his 1941 film said it all: Tall, Dark and Handsome.

the *Rockies* (1942) with Carmen Miranda, and *Wee Willie Winkie* (1937) with Shirley Temple, were his professional bread-and-butter. His film work was preceded by early success in theater, and he returned to theater late in his career. The son of wealthy Cuban émigrés, Romero was dutifully working in a New York banking job when a girlfriend suggested that they audition as nightclub performers. Following Romero's stage debut as a dancer in *Lady Do* in 1927, producer Brock Pemberton spotted him dancing at the Montmartre Club in Manhattan and cast him as Count di Ruvo in the lead of a road company production of *Strictly Dishonorable*, opposite Margaret Sullavan.

In the late-Prohibition days of the late 1920s and early thirties, Romero described himself as having "plenty of clothes and no money." Tall, mustachioed, with jet patent-leather hair and doe eyes, Romero became a skilled gate-crasher. He was so witty and fastidiously groomed that no one thought to question his credentials as the party guest whose

name no one could quite place; he was obviously supposed to be there, because his being there made the party so much more swell. He did the same with his film roles, not so much elevating them as simply lightening them, and making the audience believe that both they and he were exactly in the right place at the right time, at least until the credits rolled. He was, in the best sense, a great pretender.

Romero made his Broadway debut in *Dinner at Eight,* which ran for more than three hundred performances. More stage-roles followed, in *Stella Brady, All Points West* and *Social Register.* His film debut was in 1933 in *The Shadow Laughs.*

Romero was at his most suave opposite Marlene Dietrich in The Devil Is a Woman *(1935). As The Cisco Kid, he proved that even a hard-riding western action hero must know how to accessorize.*

Later that year, a screen test for MGM landed him a role in *The Thin Man* (1934) with William Powell and Myrna Loy, as well as a three-year contract. Working at both Fox and Warner studios, he starred in such films as *Love Before Breakfast* (1936) with Carole Lombard, *The Devil Is a Woman* with Marlene Dietrich (1935), *Captain from Castile* (1947), where he played Hernan Cortes opposite Tyrone Power, and the aptly-named *Tall, Dark and Handsome* (1941).

He was Hollywood's most highly visible, if elusive, unattached man. Of those days, he said, "Sure, I was one of those nightclub Romeos, honey. I've had all the babes out. You name 'em, Romero's dated 'em." Romero's little black book of "babes" read like a casting director's dream: he was photographed endlessly out on the town with the likes of Joan Crawford, Marlene Dietrich, Ann Sothern, Ann Sheridan, Loretta Young, Betty Furness, Claire Trevor, Sonja Henie, Alice Faye, Ann Rutherford, Carmen Miranda, Barbara Stanwyck and Betty Grable, many his co-stars. His self-styled caddishness with the fair sex, validated by flamboyant roles like *The Gay Caballero* (1940), was just another mask.

Romero was never seriously linked with any of the many women he grandly escorted around Hollywood, and never married. When he was

He was at his most relaxed in a flawless tuxedo, cocktail in hand, a gardenia on his lapel.

considered one of Hollywood's two most eligible bachelors (the other was Jimmy Stewart) in 1947, he said, "Wives—they're too much trouble. I don't know what it is with married people around this town. But something always goes sour. That's enough to scare me off."

If Romero ever had married, most of Hollywood would have arched a collective eyebrow. Throughout this career, rumors abounded of homosexual liaisons, though the press never exposed them. Later in life

Romero defined glamor, from the high gloss of his patent leather shoes to the sheen of his marcelled waves. He adopts the rugged outdoorsman look in Love Before Breakfast *(1936) with Carole Lombard.*

he spoke publicly about his gayness, even cracking the occasional joke about it on national television.

As Hollywood's most desirable dancing partner, he seemed completely at ease with the elegant clothes and the glittering nightlife, one of that nearly extinct species of man who was at his most relaxed in a flawless tuxedo, cigarette and cocktail in hand, a gardenia on his lapel

Echoing Romero's own tongue-in-cheek approach, his friends sarcastically called him "Butch."

Stardom at its glitziest seemed his natural state, as though he were a guest of honor at an unending circle of cocktail parties and A-list soirees who never had to attend to mundane matters of sleeping, sitting through meetings, paying bills, cutting the grass. Nocturnal, feline, he had no desire to convince the public that he was Everyman; after all, he wasn't. His look was way beyond dapper, going past merely stylish to stylized and razor-sharp. A part split his marcelled hair with mathemat-

ical precision, and his mustache, about which he was very vain (he refused to shave it, even for his late-career roles) was always a masterpiece of geometry. He not only wore the white tie and tails well—he wore them with authority, as though they had been invented for him.

Romero's ease with his own glamorous persona kept his arch and increasingly campy movie roles from becoming simply smarmy. That knowing smile, with one eyebrow lifted almost skeptically, not only became his trademark expression of ironic detachment, it signified disbelief at his own good fortune. Prior to his stage debut, Romero seemed destined to inherit his father's exporting firm. He shuddered to the *Los Angeles Times*, "If his business hadn't gone broke, I'd be exporting nuts, bolts and sugar machinery right now. What an awful thought."

Fox Studios fed Romero a steady stream of solidly commercial roles, including *The Little Princess* (1939) with Shirley Temple and *Tales of Manhattan (1942)* with Ginger Rogers. In 1939 he starred in *The Return*

The enthusiastic romantic, above, Romero was considered Hollywood's most desirable dance partner. Opposite, he cuts the rug with Joan Crawford at Hollywood's fabled Cocoanut Grove.

of the Cisco Kid, reprising a role which had been played by several Latin and non-Latin actors. In 1940 through 1941, Romero then made six *Cisco Kid* adventures, and for the first time in his career seemed out of place.

Perched in the saddle, it was too obvious that he was in character and in costume. He was, after all, a "Latin from Manhattan" as he liked to call himself, born in New York City in 1907. Romero's sophisticated urban image clashed with the rugged Cisco Kid role, and Darryl Zanuck at Fox dropped the series.

The 1950s found him without a contract after eighteen years with his "family" at Fox. In addition to "freelancing" himself into the casts of movies including *The Americano* (1955) with Glenn Ford and *Ocean's Eleven* (1960) alongside the Rat Pack, Romero had a successful series of dance appearances in Las Vegas. The peacock, newly humbled, admitted, "Out of shape, oh brother. I was wearing corn plasters above and below my toes, and taping my ankles twice."

Bunions aside, Romero wore his age well, his high, silver-fox hair and more-worldly-than-ever gaze allowing him to make the transition smoothly into television. His two most memorable small-screen roles, however, were wildly divergent. In the mid-sixties, he played the cackling Joker in television's high-camp "Batman" series, where he shed his tux for green hair and a purple suit. Batman himself, Adam West, remembered that

On the dance floor, Romero always dipped his ladies with Latin Lover dash.

the producers indulged Romero's refusal to shave off the memento of his most dashing movie roles, allowing him to cover it with makeup. West said, "If you look closely, you can see the mustache through the greasepaint."

Romero's "Joker" was followed by his role in another cult favorite, "Falcon Crest," where he played a Greek billionaire opposite Jane Wyman, with considerably more sartorial sense. The enchanting lounge lizard proved, surprisingly, that he was quite the chameleon.

In the seventies and eighties, bemoaning the ragged state of the movie business, he starred in a few plays, including *My Three Angels, Goodbye Tiger, Goodbye Fifi, A Dash of Spirits* and *The Max Factor*. In 1991, he accepted the Imagen Hispanic Media Award for Lifetime Achievement. Never losing his exquisitely mild wickedness or the ruse of being a ladies' man, he told the *Los Angeles Times*, "I can't date women

my own age any more—I hate going to cemeteries. So I look for the younger breed. I take them dining and dancing and by the end of an evening they're bushwacked, whereas I still want to go on to the next nightclub."

He died at the age of eighty-six, after sharing a comfortable house he had purchased with his unmarried sister in 1943. A few months prior to his death, he told interviewers that he missed Hollywood's lost elegance. He was in favor, he said, of stars keeping up appearances—he would never be a jeans and T-shirt sort of guy. "We Latins make splendid lovers and splendid older men," he said, adding, "My doctor used to tell me to slow down—at least he did until he dropped dead." Romero always chose to glide through Hollywood like a black swan, keeping his intimate life a mystery, guarded beneath the midnight sheen of his feathers. Letting it all hang out was unthinkable. Perhaps it was his secrets which made him smile that Cheshire Cat smile.❖

During World War II, Romero frequently served as a spokesman for the war effort. Above, with Carole Landis, he packs a basket for a soldier.

RICARDO
MONTALBAN

the reluctant

ROMEO

Never mind that the white suit he wore on TV's "Fantasy Island" had to be con-
structed of suffocatingly hot, heavy-duty nylon-lined polyester to keep Mr. Roarke wrin-
kle-free: Ricardo Montalban never broke a sweat. Never mind that a back injury sustained
while filming *Across the Wide Missouri* in 1951 kept him in chronic pain for decades: his
smile was always bright and convincing.

He was a trouper, a pro, the marrying kind, husband material, a deeply devout
Catholic who kept a fresh bunch of violets at his wife's bedside. He spent his career denying the obvious—that he could sing, that he could dance, that women wanted to melt into
his arms. Mothers, mothers-in-law and good girls loved him, and his all-encompassing

Ricardo Montalban brought new sophistication to the role of the Latin Lover. Although he
starred in Latin Lovers (1953), opposite, with Lana Turner, he disdained clichéd Romeo roles.

wholesomeness limited his access to Hollywood's ladder of stardom.

His soothing voice will always conjure up his thirteen years of "fine Corinthian leather" ads for Chrysler, and his television identity as the unflappable Mr. Roarke is more instantly identifiable to most Americans than his forty-plus movie roles (including thirteen films made in his native Mexico). Montalban met all the criteria needed to qualify as stereotypic ladies' man, both on- and offscreen, but he had been a painfully bashful boy back home in Torreón. And although his muscled dancer's physique,

> **Even with his shirt off, Montalban keeps the lid on the simmering pot.**

singing voice and chiseled features frequently resulted in being cast as a romantic lead, he rejected the stereotype of the Latin Lover. Even so, he starred in a 1953 release called, like it or not, *Latin Lovers,* in which he appeared with a nubile Rita Moreno, and taught Lana Turner to tango.

Studio executives made sure to capitalize upon his sex appeal as much as possible, frequently casting him in shirtless roles such as *Right Cross* (1950) in which he plays a boxer, and *My Man and I* (1952) in which he portrays a bare-chested handyman. *Right Cross,* apart from its beefcake appeal, represents a small turning point in the saga of American films starring Latin actors. Generally, the suave Latin man tempts and loses the nice white girl; however, as boxer Johnny Monterez, Montalban successfully woos and wins his Anglo trainer's daughter, played by June Allyson.

Montalban complicated the familiar Latin Lover formula by counteracting his sensual potential with an aura of steely self-control. Even with his shirt off, Montalban keeps the lid on the simmering pot, creating a sensation of sexual tension by what is not said. Montalban is the Latin Lover who always played hard to get. Unlike more overstated performers, both his ethnicity and his masculinity were kept in check.

Apart from his rejection of roles which he considered racist,

Montalban's debut in a major American film was Fiesta *(1947) with Esther Williams. This musical extravaganza led to roles with Cyd Charisse, Lana Turner, opposite in* Latin Lovers*, Ann Miller, and Shirley MacLaine.*

Montalban also refused to play the stereotypic Latin playboy in his personal life. In 1964, he told the *Los Angeles Times*, "Merchandising is a part of my business . . . I haven't done it. I have been myself, and myself is not good print . . . I still haven't gotten the part. But I might have if there had been an aura of excitement about my personal life."

In October, 1944, he eloped with Georgianna Young, the youngest sister of Loretta Young. The marriage was graced by four children, and persisted unmarred by even the slightest whiff of the sort of dirt so beloved by gossip columnists. Their circuitous path to love seemed guided by the stars. While still living in Mexico, he had seen Georgianna as a twelve-year-old bit actress in her role in *The Story of Alexander Graham Bell* (1939), which starred Don Ameche and Loretta Young. "My heart went aflutter," he recalled.

As a shy teen, while the other boys bragged about their conquests with local girls, Montalban carried a photo of the blue-eyed blonde in his wallet as though she were his *novia* (girlfriend). Then Georgianna began modeling, and her photograph appeared in fashion magazines which were delivered to the small dry goods store owned by the Montalban family.

A few years later, after moving to Hollywood, Montalban was aflutter again when he happened to glimpse Georgianna one Sunday morning at the Church of the Good Shepherd in Beverly Hills. After services he followed her in his car, but the young actress turned a corner, and disappeared from his life once again.

Working with director Norman Foster, Montalban met the director's wife, Sally Blaine, who was another sister of Loretta Young. Sally invited Montalban to a cocktail party where he finally came face-to-face with Georgianna, now eighteen. Of their meeting, he said, "Of course, I knew right there, that was it." They were secretly married two weeks later in Tijuana, and the mar-

MGM called the tango the "most romantic dance in history." Jane Powell and Montalban prove it in Two Weeks with Love *(1950).*

riage endured through the decades which followed without a single separation, public spat or rumored indiscretion. Meanwhile, industry cynics continued to whisper that it was too good to be true, hoping for a spicy scrap of scandal which never came.

The Montalban marriage was the stuff of the sweetest, yearning *norteño*, the diametric opposite of dirty laundry which seemed to give actors added star-power in Hollywood. Of course, a different sort of man would have hunted down his intended, using his own career cachet and his relationship with the Foster-Blaines as necessary means to reach Georgianna's bed. It is telling that Montalban did not—and, miraculously, she came to him anyway. The studios tried their best to cast him as a wolf, but in a twist which may have compromised his career, he was in fact a lamb in *lobo's* clothing.

Montalban's easy transition from an ethnic perception to a broader persona makes sense in light of his personal history. He was born in Mexico City in 1920 and raised in Torreón, the son of Castilian émigrés. His older brother Carlos, who was acting in Spanish-language movies for Fox Studios, sent seventeen-year-old Ricardo a plane ticket to Los Angeles and introduced him to his professional dance partner of the time, a striking Latina named Marguerita Cansino (later known as Rita Hayworth). Ricardo was starstruck but Carlos insisted that he complete his education or be sent home to Torreón. Ricardo complied.

Studio talent scouts screen-tested Ricardo upon his graduation, and Carlos then took him to Cedarhurst, New York, to meet Tallulah Bankhead who was casting a summer-stock play called *Her Cardboard Lover*. Bankhead auditioned the younger Montalban in her hotel room while her famous pet lion cub flossed its fangs on his shoe. He

recalled to *TV Guide* in 1979, "I think I got the part because Miss Bankhead decided that if I could retain my composure under such circumstances, it was probable that I would be able to remember my lines."

His career as a romantic lead was on the brink of being launched. However, Montalban spurned the obvious path, setting the pattern of striving within his career. In 1941, he returned to Mexico to make films, preferring the meaty dramatic roles he was offered there to the fluffy, song-and-dance parts now being sent his way in the States. He became Mexico's most prominent actor, and his performance in *Santa* (1943) won him the equivalent of an Academy Award nomination.

Montalban helped to form *Nosotros* ("We") in 1969, an organization which dedicates itself to ridding film and television of degrading Latino roles. In 1978, he was cast in the lead of ABC's enormously successful weekly series, "Fantasy Island," a role in which he was neither identified as Latin, nor asked to play an overheated lover. But the role brought the actor mass-market exposure not possible in motion pictures.

He also found a surprising niche in science fiction, starring in the wildly commercial *Planet of the Apes* sequels throughout the seventies. Then in 1982, he donned a shredded blond wig (which made him look like an elegantly wasted rock star) to play the archvillain in the film *Star Trek II: The Wrath of Khan*. The grandly literate Khan (he quotes Milton and Melville) was a role that finally allowed Montalban to defy his old Latin Lover casting, even if he had to travel all the way to another galaxy to do it.

Montalban, unlike Khan, is too much of a gentleman to become bitter. Instead, he has made a career of counting his blessings. Of his image as a sex symbol, Montalban shrugged, "I get fan mail, and some of it does refer to it. But sex appeal, I don't know what it is—I don't think I have it. Maybe that in itself becomes endearing."❖

Montalban downplayed his sex appeal, setting his sights for meatier dramatic roles. However, with Shelley Winters in My Man and I *(1952), his taut physique did most of the talking.*

FERNANDO LAMAS

featherweight FANDANGO

I've played the same stupid role for the last seven or eight years," Fernando Lamas complained to the *Los Angeles Mirror* in 1961, "They seem to think all Latins make love all day long. I assure you that isn't true. Once in a while I read a book!"

Didst the man protest too much? In many ways, Fernando Lamas seemed among the least complicated of Latin Lovers, always utterly at home in his long, elegant skin, whether swimming beside Esther Williams (whom he would later marry), or smoothing out the rough edges of a dubious script with a convenient song sung in his easy baritone. He danced as effortlessly as he hit a tennis ball, with offhand finesse. As he himself wrote of his character Count Danilo in *The Merry Widow* (1952), "Women swayed reedlike before

Fernando Lamas made it all look easy, whether bursting into effortless song or capturing Lana Turner's heart, opposite, in The Merry Widow.

his breezy charm." Yet, in 1978, he was still complaining, this time to the *Los Angeles Times*: "I couldn't break the Latin Lover image, hard as I tried. It was a great image to have off the screen, but a pain in the ass in the movies."

He is most readily remembered for his graceful, Apollonian frame (he had been a prize-winning boxer and swimmer in his native Argentina), for the aristocracy of his aquiline features, and for his many splashy romances with his co-stars in gossamer-weight Hollywood vehicles.

Lamas frequently became romantically linked—sometimes in matrimony—to the women with whom he appeared on-camera, yet he bridled at the suggestion that his shared scenes automatically led to shared sheets. In 1953, he insisted, "It is not by my plan that I work again and again with the ladies important in my personal life. It is circumstantial." With no other leading man has this seemed more true: the determining circumstance surrounding Lamas' life was simply that women, his co-stars included, found it impossible to resist him. Was he to blame? He seemed as helpless in its grasp as they were.

Born in 1915 in Buenos Aires, he described his childhood as "lonely," having lost both parents before the age of four. He had been raised by a stern grandmother and aunt, perhaps preparing him for a lifetime of analyzing female moods and behavior. Lamas had been an established stage, screen and radio star both in Latin America and in Europe, including a role in *Historia De Una Mala Mujer* opposite Dolores Del

Among Lamas' four brides were Arlene Dahl, above right, in 1954, and Esther Williams (above, scrutinizing Lana Turner's jewels) in 1967. Lamas always seemed at home, whether taking in a Tijuana bullfight with starlet Diane Smith, (opposite) or bantering over cocktails with a leading lady.

Rio, before his arrival in Hollywood in 1950, the year he signed with MGM. Before leaving Argentina, he had appeared in a total of twenty-one films, starring in nineteen of these, always as the villain.

Once in Hollywood, Lamas reinvented himself, this time as a romantic leading man, and his new life took many impetuous turns. Ten days after meeting Lana Turner at the premiere of *Quo Vadis*, the two were making headlines. Turner was subsequently credited with helping to launch Lamas' career in American films, particularly in his being cast as her leading man in *The Merry Widow*.

Women swayed reedlike before his breezy charm.

They were a gilded if not golden couple, both before the cameras and in the popular imagination if not in real life. Public knowledge of their affair seemed to make their on-screen love scenes glow with genuine heat. Turner protested vigorously whenever the columnists linked her with any other man, and Lamas refused a role in *Sombrero* (1953) because the Mexican location would have taken him from her side. The inevitable accusations followed, insinuating that Lamas was merely a playboy-opportunist who attached himself to powerful and influential women to further his own career.

The bond proved as fleeting as it was fiery. By October, 1952, the engagement was off. Accounts of the split vary, but most agree that the romance ended at a party held by Marion Davies for singer Johnnie Ray. When movie-Tarzan Lex Barker asked Turner to dance, an altercation apparently followed, and the gaucho and the blonde were no more. Following the breakup, Lamas was promptly dropped from Turner's next picture *Latin Lovers* (1953), and was replaced by the more earnest Ricardo Montalban.

Lamas then described his 1952 role of Count Danilo in *The Merry Widow* as the favorite acting assignment of his career, not because of his involvement with Turner, but because it ". . . helped me get better acquainted with Arlene Dahl." Lamas and the red-tressed Dahl had met long before Lana Turner entered the picture: Lamas' first screen test had been opposite Dahl, when Dahl still was married to Lex Barker. With the

Preceding page, Lamas and Lana Turner in The Merry Widow *(1952). Chic, relaxed Lamas' knew the fan-magazine potential of a barechested kiss photograph. This one is from* Sangaree *(1953).*

perfect symmetry found only in the Hollywood tabloids, Barker and Turner became an item simultaneously with Lamas and Dahl, shortly after the Barker-Dahl divorce.

The marriage lasted five years, ending after one film together (*Sangaree*, 1953), one public separation and reconciliation, and the birth of one child, Lorenzo (now himself a nineties-style television Latin Lover of considerable smolder). Dahl never disclosed specifics of their divorce, except to say "there are so many reasons you couldn't print them all."

Lamas had admitted to reporters that his temper "interferes with things sometimes"—hardly surprising from the man who had also said in 1951, "In this country, you make love more calmly. You are tender and say endearing things to a woman. But Latins are hot-tempered. We grab a girl around the neck, grasp her arms until they are black-and-blue and shred her clothing."

In 1967 (and again in 1969), he was once more linked with a successful woman, this time his co-star in the silly *Dangerous When Wet* (1953). The woman was Esther Williams, who became the fourth and most enduring Mrs. Lamas. They remained married until Lamas' death. He attributed the longevity of their marriage to Williams' innate goodness, saying, "She is the most tender woman in the entire world. I don't know how she got so tender, but I have a hunch it's all that chlorine."

Initially, he had hesitated to tell the studio biographers of his competitive swimming awards in Argentina, since "It came to me in a flash that if they knew I swam, they'd stick me in Esther Williams movies. I didn't want to wind up being Nelson Eddy to her Jeanette MacDonald

Two masterpieces of Latin design—Lamas and then-wife Arlene Dahl get up-close and personal in front of the Coliseum in Rome.

in a swimming pool." Although Lamas denied exerting any pressure upon his new wife to remove herself from his industry, Williams retired from the screen soon after the wedding.

Lamas wore his advancing age well, time only sharpening his regal bone structure and adding insouciance to his smooth, seductively jaded persona. He settled into "continental" roles of indeterminate ethnicity, directed over sixty television episodes (including the long-running soap "Falcon Crest" in which his son Lorenzo starred) and appeared in several low-budget Italian productions. On "Saturday Night Live," Billy Crystal immortalized him to a new generation in the form of the comedic character "Fernando," the ascoted silver fox who would address the screen with a convincing, "You look *mah-velous*!" often followed by "And it is so much more important to look mah-velous than to feel mah-velous."

In 1982, Lamas left the set of his new television series, "Gavilan," complaining of back pain; cancer took his life a month later, at the age of sixty-seven. Denial had always been the defining element in Lamas' appeal: denial of what was painful, denial of what was ugly, denial of the passage of time itself. He persisted in denying the obvious with the media throughout his career, insisting to *Look* magazine in 1952, "I'm serious about my career as an actor. I sure don't think I'm any God's-gift-to-women." ❖

DESI ARNAZ

hurricane in the

HIPS

His good looks, a refined blend of Spanish, Irish, French and Cuban bloodlines, rivaled that of any Hollywood headliner, and his social pedigree outclassed every major star's. Yet his beauty and aristocracy only partially explain the appeal of conga-king Desi Arnaz—his aura of danger raised the nation's body temperature, and set off a fever on the dance floors of every major city in the U.S. in the 1940s.

His power as a performer rested on one simple fact: Desi moved his hips. His sensual gyrations were a shock to the nation, especially since, in the 1930s, white America denied life below the waist. The lower body, with its shameful cravings and awful consequences, was best ignored; that way, those hips would cause the least trouble. So the arch and shimmy

Charisma, Cubanismo and sheer joy made Desi Arnaz captivating on-stage. He introduced the conga line to the U.S., and was by far the sexiest TV husband of the 1950s.

of Desi's pelvis, powered by the syncopated rhythms of his tall congas, electrified the country much the way Elvis would in the fifties and the Twist would in the sixties. Men and women, Latin and Anglo alike, went wild when a lock of Arnaz's wet, raven hair tumbled forward as his hands flew over the taut drumheads, grazing his sweating, elegant brow, and his hips began to sway. The orchestra would spin out the melody in the wake of his rhythms, which gradually grew in complexity, recklessness and speed, like a tropical storm gathering momentum. His sheer abandon was unknown to mainstream American audiences, except those who had ventured "to Harlem in ermine and pearls" to witness African-American blues and jazz musicians in the uptown night spots.

Prior to fleeing Cuba during the 1933 Machado Revolution, the cosmopolitan and wealthy Arnaz family had been influential in Spain and Cuba for centuries. Desi exhibited all the characteristics that Cubans of the forties associated with a distinguished legacy: pale skin, flawless fine features, perfect teeth and a well-bred, civilized demeanor. But what he unleashed in audiences, especially in women, was purely wild. He wasn't a tortured, brooding sulker like Valentino or a strutting rooster like Gilbert Roland. His sexuality was exuberant, natural and joyous. Desi was kinetic, fearless in much the same way a great athlete is fearless. As a performer, he was willing to surrender control, making his performances edgy, thrilling and cathartic.

> ## Desi was kinetic, fearless in much the same way a great athlete is fearless.

For Arnaz, there was no rupture between his privileged upbringing as Desiderio Alberto Arnaz y de Acha III and his uninhibited interpretation of traditional Cuban rhythms. Of his Miami audition for the legendary band leader Xavier Cugat, he wrote, "My Cuban blood was flowing. My hips were revolving, my feet were kicking, my arms were waving. It would have made Elvis Presley look as if he were standing still."

Arnaz's savage side attracted Lucille Ball. Later she admitted, "Eloping with Desi was the most daring thing I ever did in my life. I never fell

Barely out of his teens, Arnaz, opposite with conga, became one of the hottest tickets in the country. His "Babalu" led to Desilu and mega-stardom.

in love with anyone quite so fast. He was very handsome and romantic. But he also frightened me, he was so wild. I knew I shouldn't have married him, but that was one of the biggest attractions." The pair had met while filming his first movie, the 1940 RKO production of *Too Many Girls*. The columnists predicted the marriage would last six months; in 1956, Lucy herself snorted, "Six months? I gave it six weeks."

In *Too Many Girls*, Desi sang the big production number wreathed in a hoop of leaping flames—literally a torch song. The aptly-named title song also provided an appropriately fiery personification for Desi's effect upon club-goers.

Even though few if any *norte americanos* would have recognized the motifs as specifically African, the unmistakable use of polyrhythmic percussive techniques in Cuban dance music made the island sexually bewitching as well as a happy place

The body became fluid, the knees bent, the dance settled warmly just below the navel.

of cigars, sunshine and rum drinks (classically given their supernatural strength with Bacardi rum, a company co-founded by Desi's maternal grandfather Alberto Acha). In the forties, jazz aficionados dug the West African "hooks" in the form of "Cubop," or Cuban-styled be-bop. In the more pop vein, Xavier Cugat, Cachao (Israel Lopez, father of the mambo) and Desi Arnaz, had mainstream America doing things with its hips which would have seemed positively indecent a decade earlier. Even the 1920s Charleston, for all of its reported shock value, was a

Arnaz began playing the guitar in Cuba, above. In Cuban Pete *(1946) opposite, he serenaded little Beverly Simmons who appeared in the film.*

rigid, jerking dance comprised of stiff legs and a stiffer body, just as the flapper's supposedly scandalous frock actually disguised the perilous curves of her flesh. The dance moves associated with the music of Cuba were just the opposite. The body became fluid, the knees bent, and the emphasis in terms of dance rose from the feet and settled warmly just below the navel. The torso, especially the lower torso, became the focus.

This provocatively Caribbean invitation to twitch and swirl the pelvis, even delicately at first, made Cuba seem a far more wonderfully dangerous place than, say, Italy or France, where the gigolos were slick, but reassuringly Caucasian. Although Desi himself was the fairest of the fair in ethnic terms, his hands brought forward the voices of the *orishas*, the Yoruban spirits. America quickly learned that Cuba was unmistakably the real tropics, not St. Tropez. The ancient call of the drum, echoing all the way from Mother Africa to the Caribbean to Miami to New York and Hollywood, made Cuba synonymous with jungle fever.

Later, in the 1950s and 1960s, white recording artists of the most witheringly bland ilk—Pat Boone comes to mind—introduced middle-class teenagers to musically emaciated versions of songs written and performed by African-American artists and released only as "race records." This reinterpretation was necessary, because "race records" never received airplay in major markets. Desi did the same, although with far more artistry and authenticity, removing African music from its threatening associations. He brought rhythm to the

foreground, placing melody second, and America leaped to its feet as though just awakened from a deep slumber.

Bing Crosby recognized the equation instantly. A week after graduating from high school, Desi reported to work for Cugie at the Waldorf-Astoria Hotel in New York. The following week, he opened at Billy Rose's Aquacade in Cleveland, a prime venue of its day. The next gig took Arnaz to the Arrowhead Inn, a posh gambling casino in Saratoga, New York, where he was introduced to Bing. Bing greeted Desi in Spanish, sang *"Quieréme Mucho"* with him, then chastized Cugie for only paying the youngster thirty dollars a week. "Give him a raise," he said. "One of these days, you're going to be asking him for a job."

Desi introduced the first conga line to the United States at the posh Park Central bistro in Miami, creating near-riots every night. For months on end, the club was packed to crush-capacity until dawn as revelers flocked to the bar to ease their thirst, and returned again and again to the dance floor to be pummeled by the insistent drumbeat.

Desi was the hottest property on the national night-club circuit, guaranteeing standing-room-only crowds wherever he played. In a stroke of marketing genius, he was cast in the 1939 Broadway version of the Rodgers and Hart musical, *Too Many Girls*, and the role was carried to film the following year. The attraction between Desi and a former Goldwyn Girl and RKO contract player, Lucille Ball, was instant, their mutual attraction almost palpable on screen.

Their pairing also was a publicist's dream. Lucy (Desi refused to call her Lucille) was several years older than Desi, perilously close to thirty. Being linked with the Cuban fireball breathed new life into her tottering box-office allure, giving

Preceding page, Arnaz liberated the hips of America. Then came his fiery film debut in Too Many Girls *(1940) with Lucille Ball and Ann Miller.*

publicity momentum to a film which would otherwise have been strictly a boilerplate Hollywood musical. Lucy stares into the camera while Desi gazes into her famous saucer-eyes, or deeply buries his face in the bouquet of her neck and hair. Of the duo, the press chief of RKO admitted at the time: "Except for fashion layouts and leg art in the fan magazines, we'd always had a problem getting publicity for Lucy . . . Then along comes Desi, who's not a big star, but very promising, very handsome, and very sexy. So they're not exactly Gable and Lombard, but you can still get a helluva lot of coverage."

Their relationship was a consuming, devouring burn. Tap-queen Ann Miller, co-starring in *Too Many Girls*, commented "They were absolutely together night and day. They were enraptured of each other, which is putting it mildly." Then the separations which would plague their marriage began. After the seven-week shoot of *Too Many Girls* wrapped, Lucy was committed to stay in Los Angeles to begin a new picture, *A Girl, A Guy and a Gob (1941),* while Desi had agreed to rejoin the stage company of *Too Many Girls* in Chicago. Lucy's grueling shooting schedule often prevented her from joining Desi for his all-night *descargos* (jam sessions) at places like the Palladium, Trocadero, Casa Mañana, Florentine Gardens, Cocoanut Grove and El Zerape, and she worried about the long-legged glamor girls who filled those Latin clubs each night.

In November, 1940, they eloped to Greenwich, Connecticut. Because the civil ceremony took place on a Sunday, Lucy's ring was from the five-and-dime. Although it turned her finger green, and although Desi replaced it with other, more precious bands in the years which followed, Lucy never took it off. News of the union preceded them back to New York, and the Roxy Theater was shoulder-to-shoulder in a standing ovation when Desi appeared on stage with his new bride for his evening's first set. Fire marshals stood in the aisles to contain capacity crowds that filled all four tiers of the huge theater, jamming the aisles. Theater management had provided the mob with packets of rice that rained down upon Desi and Lucy like a snowstorm of wedding wishes.

Like a tropical monsoon, their heat stirred trouble. They fought constantly about infidelities, real or imagined. Desi was in a poor position to defend himself, since the columnists enjoyed portraying him as a playboy. In a similar vein, Lucy was required by the studio publicity departments to be glimpsed at premieres and parties with her male co-stars, to generate interest in her films. To which Desi replied, "Then quit the f**king film business and just be my wife. I don't like you being seen around town with any other man than me. I have not become that Americanized yet."

Desi gave Hollywood's gossip mongers little to work with regarding his roving eye, although he did later write in his autobiography, *A Book*, "I must admit that I was an old-fashioned Latin, raised observing and believing in the classic double standard . . . Your fooling around can in no way affect your love for (your wife). That relationship is sacred and a few peccadilloes mean nothing. Lucy knew this."

Perhaps, but she filed for divorce from Desi for the first time in September of 1944, citing mental cruelty as the cause (the divorce was quickly called off). The clearly passionate couple wanted a baby, yet conception was mysteriously elusive. Desi's mother reminded them that their civil ceremony may have satisfied the requirements of the state, but that they were not truly man and wife in the eyes of God without a sacramental marriage. She suggested that perhaps the Almighty was withholding His blessing until the union was sanctified. The couple held a lavish church wedding in 1949, for more than sentimental reasons. Soon after Desi and Lucy's Roman Catholic ceremony, their daughter Lucie was conceived, followed by "little Ricky," Desi, Jr.

The marriage lasted until 1960 when they divorced. The love between them, however, seemed to persist until the end of their lives, even when each remarried. For fifteen years after their divorce, Desi sent Lucy red and white carnations on the date of their wedding anniversary. In 1963, when Desi married Edith Mack Hirsch, Lucy sent the newlyweds a giant horseshoe of flowers with a card reading "You both picked a winner."

The volatility of the relationship ultimately was its downfall. The clash was essentially a class conflict. In spite of his foreign-ness, Desi was clearly the highbrow. Desi could not help but exude his aristocracy, even when clowning as the white-tuxed Ricky Ricardo. Today, Arnaz Drive in Beverly Hills is not named for Desi as most locals would believe, but rather for his prestigious heritage. In 1869, Isabella, Queen of Spain, appointed his great-grandfather, Don Manuel II, to be mayor of Santiago de Cuba and granted the family several pieces of land in Southern California. His grandfather, Don Desiderio, was the Cuban doctor assigned to Teddy Roosevelt's Rough Riders when they went up San Juan Hill during the Spanish-American War, and Desi's own father was the youngest mayor in Santiago's history.

The family lost its fortune during the Revolution, and Desi liked to joke that he was a "Cuban bird-cage cleaner," a job he in fact held when he was in high school in Miami. His breeding still placed him in a Henry Higgins role with Lucy. On TV Ricky made no attempt to civilize Lucy; it would have been beneath him. His utter exasperation with her, and her zany scrambling to keep just a catastrophe or two ahead of his elite disdain, is the winning formula of "I Love Lucy." In a surprising reversal, it is finally the Anglo-Saxon Lucy (Ricardo, *nee* McGillicuddy) who is in fact the savage.

Desi's rare films included *Four Jacks and a Jill* (1941), *Father Takes A*

Wife (1941), *The Navy Comes Through* (1942), *Bataan* (1943), *Cuban Pete* (1946) and *Holiday in Havana* (1949), but he lost his footing once removed from the musical setting. In spite of the fact that Desi was as photogenic as human physiology could permit, his lack of dramatic nuance and thick accent made it impossible for him to make the transition into screen roles which did not involve the conga drums.

When Lucy proposed that Desi be cast as her mate in the televised version of her CBS radio series, "My Favorite Husband," studio executives dismissed the notion because they "didn't look married." Of course, this case of life imitating art became the basis for "I Love Lucy" and the formidable Desilu empire, created largely through Desi's infallible business sense.

Desi persuaded CBS to record the show in Hollywood, before live studio audiences, back in the days when shows were shot live in New York. This shift revolutionized the television industry—Desi had literally invented the rerun, and thus kicked off the multi-billion dollar concept of syndication—and made Desi and Lucy the highest-paid entertainers in television history. In 1957, they sold RKO Studios the rights to their show and purchased the studio for six million dollars; a few years after the initial airings of "I Love Lucy," Desi sold back the one hundred and eighty episodes to CBS for a reported four and one-half million dollars.

In addition to the weekly half-hours of "I Love Lucy," Desi also showcased the unstoppable formula in thirteen monthly hour-long episodes of "The Lucy and Desi

Arnaz' lighthearted clowning masked a shrewd business savvy. Many of his innovations as a producer—filming shows before a live studio audience, for instance—shaped the television industry as we know it today.

Comedy Hour." The last of these, "Lucy Meets the Mustache," was also the last of the Arnaz marriage. The pair had denied the rumored split, but at last the truth surfaced and the Cuban and the redhead were no more.

In 1962, Desi sold his share of the company back to Lucy. He went on to produce television shows, breed horses and teach film classes at California State University at San Diego. Before his death of lung cancer at the age of sixty-nine in 1986, Desi told the press, "The audience knew we loved each other. Underneath all that crap was that Lucy and Ricky loved each other." ❖

OOH-LA-LA

the French

KISS

France is the northernmost edge of the Latin world. French culture has historically separated itself from its British and German neighbors by its sophisticated sensuality; *haute cuisine* and *haute couture* are expressions of France's Latin soul in highly refined form.

Likewise, the allure of France's leading men is intellectualized. Raw fleshiness is not the French way; even blunt sex is distanced by the haze of Galoise or Gitanes, and philosophical conversation. The prototype for the French lover in the golden era was Charles Boyer, who projected a luscious melancholy through what can only be called bedroom eyes.

Boyer was not a young man when he began his work in American films, nor was he tall, nor was he slender; some claim that he wore a toupee in addition to elevator shoes

Alain Delon was the quintessential bad boy of French cinema, often playing the angel-faced gangster. Chevalier was almost too French to be true (shown admiring friend Marlene Dietrich's cleavage).

and a corset (he admitted to wearing a hairpiece in a dramatic reading of Shaw's *Don Juan in Hell*).

Even given these intrusions of reality, Boyer's place in the lover's pantheon is unique. Boyer was far from leather and leaping flames: he was cognac and cream. He projected a slightly bruised romantic tenderness which seemed to promise a *soignée* mid-life love that would dry all tears, making him a favorite among movie-going women of a certain age.

Charles Boyer (as Pepe le Moko) never uttered the immortal line, "Come weez me to zee Casbah" to Hedy Lamarr in the film *Algiers* (1938). "It has dogged me for years," the Frenchman noted in 1960. "Pepe le Moko never said, 'Come with me to the Casbah.' It was probably some radio or nightclub comedian imitating my accent." And he added, "The public has an image of me as a lover, playboy, and seducer, while I have an image of myself as a serious actor. I hope we can get together some day."

He was a serious lover off-screen. He took his own life in 1978 at the age of seventy-eight, two days after the death of his wife of forty-four years, British actress Patricia Paterson. Boyer had vowed that he would never marry, but he and Paterson eloped after a whirlwind romance. Her death literally ended his life, so intense was his love for her.

Equally intense about his work—a career that lasted nearly sixty years—he started acting as a child. Born in Figeac, France, in 1899, the son of a farm machinery dealer, Boyer staged and rehearsed his own plays in his father's granary as a boy. Later, he studied philosophy at the Sorbonne and the Paris Conservatory, and his work in plays, including singing parts which showcased his excellent voice,

Charles Boyer gets nuzzled by Olivia de Havilland, while Paulette Goddard clings to his shoulder in The Constant Nymph *(1942); right, with Danielle Darieux* The Mayerling *(1936), top, with Irene Dunne in* Love Affair *(1939).*

led to early success in the theater.

His film debut was in 1920, but French film directors did not consider him sufficiently photogenic. Initially, Boyer worked for MGM in the French-language versions of English-language hits, in the years before dubbing. He starred opposite Claudette Colbert in *The Man From Yesterday* (1932), his first major role in English, and a nation of moviegoers sank into his deeply sensuous voice and wistful eyes. He became one of the most popular leading men in Hollywood, playing opposite the most desirable leading actresses, including Katharine Hepburn, Marlene Dietrich, Loretta Young, Irene Dunne, Greta Garbo, Bette Davis, Rita Hayworth, Ingrid Bergman and Jennifer Jones, in addition to Lamarr and Colbert.

Because Boyer's star appeal was never dependent upon youthfulness, his audience grew even more loyal with age. By 1946, Boyer had become the highest-paid actor on the Warner lot, raking in $207,500 in salary that year. Boyer was featured in American radio during the 1950s, and in 1951 formed the *"Four Star Playhouse"* television anthology program with Dick Powell, David Niven and Ida Lupino. His array of films includes *Fanny* (1961) with Maurice Chevalier and Horst Buchholst, *Is Paris Burning?* (1966) with Alain Delon, *Barefoot in the Park* (1967), *The Madwoman of Chaillot* (1969), *Lost Horizon* (1972) and many others.

The Boyers' only child, twenty-one-year old Michael, took his own life in 1965 by playing Russian roulette after his fiancée had broken their engagement. Following Michael's death, Boyer became increasingly reclusive, sharing the privacy of his Arizona home with his cherished wife, violin and several cats.

Boyer's most famous contemporary was Maurice Chevalier, known in France by the end of his long life as *le grandpere eternel*—the eternal grandpa. And that is the image most Americans have of Chevalier. They remember his vaudevillian vocabulary of stagy facial expressions—the slightly protruding lower lip, half-petulant, half-teasing—and his straw hat and cane, all relics from *belle epoque* Paris nightlife.

Chevalier's most memorable performance, his jaunty version of "Thank Heaven for Little Girls" in *Gigi* (1958), complete with suggestive eye-rolling and smarmy winks, would today trigger a firestorm of criticism. Chevalier would have been shocked to learn that any audience heard literal, lurid insinuations in his song. He was a *boulevardier*, to be sure, but American audiences loved him because he possessed a kind of rakish courtliness. He became the twinkly, septuagenarian Gallic charmer who could cause any *grandmere* to blush when she saw his pictures at the local *bijou*.

Colette wrote in her memoirs, "Maurice Chevalier is a tall young

man who walks like a boneless human snake. His fists are too heavy for his frail wrists. Indeed, he is a fragile being, dumb and ever-conscious of his loneliness, and with an anxious, wandering pale-blue gaze which tells of acute neurasthenia."

Many years before Chaplin called himself the Little Tramp, Chevalier called himself the Little Chevalier, dressed in a buffoonish costume. By 1910, he was appearing at the Folies-Bergeres opposite a woman who was to quickly become his mistress though she was twenty

Maurice Chevalier may have thanked heaven for little girls, but he positively glowed in the presence of grown women. And when the woman was Jeanette MacDonald in The Merry Widow, *opposite, a gallant nonpareil.*

years his senior, the notorious *demimondaine* "La Miss" or Mistinguette. Mistinguette was one of a handful of avant-garde cabaret performers who introduced *valse chaloupee*, also known as *dans de apache*, or apache-dancing.

Chevalier claimed that his affair with Mistinguette was his once-in-a-lifetime love. Mistinguette soon brought Chevalier into her scandalous nightly show with Max Dearly at the Eldorado, and his career was ignited.

After the war, Chevalier donned a tux and became the symbol of Gay Paree at her most effervescent. When La Miss jilted him, he was devastated, and by 1921 was close to a break-down, feeling suicidal, blacking out and experiencing attacks of vertigo. During one performance, Chevalier forgot his lines and froze onstage, unable to speak. A young chorine named Yvonne Vallee helped him offstage, and they were married in 1927; the following year, Chevalier signed a Hollywood contract, and the newlyweds left for America where Chevalier was to appear in *Innocents of Paris* (1929). The marriage was founded in compassion, but not compatibility, so Chevalier had long affairs with Marlene Dietrich, Kay Francis, Nita Raya, Janie Michels and the "Ebony Venus" Josephine Baker, who later fingered him as a Nazi collaborator.

After his debut in *Innocents of Paris,* he made some of his best-received films in the late twenties and early 1930s, including *The Love Parade* (1929), *The Big Pond* (1930), *The Smiling Lieutenant* (1931) and *The Merry Widow* (1934). By 1934, at the age of forty-six, he was known as "the greatest male attraction in the world." Once divorced, Chevalier did not remarry. He told the press in 1964, "I have had passions for women at several times of my life . . . and when the time was coming that it made my work in danger, then I was always strong enough to resist my passion and run away bleeding like a horse but running away."

He was not modest about his stature as a performer, pointing out that no French performer since Sarah Bernhardt had commanded such a large international following.

Chevalier's career was interrupted twice more, when he was under suspicion as a collaborator in World War II, and when he turned his back on show business after his old friend and lover Marlene Dietrich was banned as "box-office poison." The lure of the stage was great, however, and he returned to please crowds from Paris to Poughkeepsie with his half-sung, half-spoken renderings (he knew his voice was creaky) of sentimental songs like "Louise" and "I Remember It Well."

The New Wave leading man needed to be deeply troubled.

In 1957, after a long absence from Hollywood, he made *Love in the Afternoon* with Gary Cooper and Audrey Hepburn, followed by *Gigi* the next year, two perennial favorites among American audiences. After an unsuccessful suicide attempt in 1971, Chevalier died the following year, as much a studio fantasy of Frenchness as he had ever been.

The notion of French romanticism as synthesized by Hollywood—can-can dancers, misty scenes of the Eiffel Tower, bad versions of "*La Vie En Rose*"—was met only with scorn by *le nouvelle vague*—the French New Wave. Actors like Jean-Paul Belmondo and Alain Delon defied the conventional notions of what it meant to be a leading man. The bridge between Boyer and Chevalier and the new breed was Louis Jourdan, nearly too handsome, but too restless for the studios' stereotyping. In 1960, Jourdan told *Coronet* magazine, "I didn't want to be perpetually cooing in a lady's ear. There's not much aesthetic satisfaction in it."

His clashes with producer David O. Selznick, who had summoned him from France to Hollywood in 1947 to make Alfred Hitchcock's *The Paradine Case* (1948), suspended him four times for his insolence. Darryl Zanuck later bought out Jourdan's contract, casting him with Debra Paget in *Bird of Paradise* (a 1951 Technicolor film extravaganza shot in

Louis Jourdan starred with Joan Fontaine in Letter From an Unknown Woman *(1948). He complained that his good looks stood in his way.*

Hawaii, which features a bare-chested Jourdan in a loincloth) and *Anne of the Indies* (1951).

Jourdan won American hearts as the Parisian bon vivant in *Gigi* (1958), and from then on considered his perfect bone structure a handicap. (In 1959, Jourdan was voted "the most exciting man in the world" by the Models League of America.) *Gigi* won him a tremendous American following, but Jourdan was often dissatisfied with the offers for slick continentals which followed.

Jourdan was smooth, elegant and mannered; the new leading man needed to be rough, tough, or at least deeply troubled. Jourdan hungered to play complicated, unsympathetic antiheroes, and was successfully cast as the villain in *Julie* (1956) opposite Doris Day, and as the evil Kamal in the James Bond thriller *Octopussy* (1983). He told the press in 1980, "I am not the character I played in *Gigi*, and if I thought I was what people think I am, I would go into the sea and never come back . . .."

The two bad boys of the French New Wave seem polar opposites—Alain Delon, with an angelic choirboy's face gone bad (he was, in fact, the lead soprano at one of the schools for wayward boys he attended), and Jean-Paul Belmondo with the broken nose and blank, defiant stare of a petty thug. Viewed together, they are the yin and yang of France's bleakest modernity: narcissistic, cynical, without the barest trace of the gentility that defined the previous generation of leading men. Cinematic scions of Bogart, their style was compared with that of Marlon Brando and James Dean; their Frenchness gave them an even more merciless, imperious edge.

Born in 1935 in the gritty Paris suburb of Sceaux, Delon quickly became the highest-paid movie star in France, although films like *Purple Noon* (1960) and *Rocco and his Brothers* (1960), the latter directed by Luchino

Visconti, received only minimal exposure in the United States. Delon resented being called "the French James Dean." In fact, Delon projected none of Dean's humanity as a counterpoint to his adolescent surliness.

After his dishonorable discharge from the French marine corps, Delon returned to France in 1955, where he is reported to have mooched a gigolo's life off wealthy socialites. On a whim, he attended the Cannes Film Festival in a borrowed suit. He was spotted that night by a Selznick talent scout, whisked to Rome to dine with Selznick, Rock Hudson and Jennifer Jones, screen-tested the next day and was offered a seven-year contract on the condition that he learn English. Instead, in a pivotal (some would say self-sabotaging) career move, Delon opted to remain in France and work with director Yves Allegret.

His film debut was in Allegret's *When the Woman Butts In* (1957), followed by several other small roles. *Rocco and his Brothers* elicited a barrage of criticism for its explicit (for the time) sex and violence, and the film made Delon an international star. After the

1963 release of *Any Number Can Win*, the biggest money-maker in French film history for many years, Delon was able to command more than one hundred fifty thousand dollars per picture.

Early in his career, Delon carried on a six-year affair with Romy Schneider, who often optimistically introduced Delon as her future husband. He ended their relationship and won the hearts of male chauvinists everywhere by leaving her a red rose and a note which read simply, *"Je regrette."* In 1964, Delon married Francine Canovas (professionally known as Nathalie Barthelemy), and their brief union produced a son, Anthony. The couple was rumored to participate in orgies with heads of state, allegedly photographed by Delon's bodyguard, Stefan Markovic.

Alain Delon kept company with an impish Jane Fonda, above, in Joy House *(1964). In almost every role he played the cold, detached lover.*

By 1968, the Delons had separated, and Nathalie was intimately involved with Markovic. Later that year, his body was found in a garbage dump near Versailles.

Delon was in St. Tropez at the time, playing a murderer in *The Swimming Pool* (1969). Markovic's murder has not been solved, although Delon's extensive contacts in the Marseilles-Corsican underworld were revealed.

A decade-long relationship with French actress Mireille Darc followed, and in 1994, Delon's companion, the Dutch ex-model Rosalie Van Breeman, gave birth to their son Alain-Fabien. In 1979, he told the *Los Angeles Times*, "I am not sure I believe in love. Not really. Passion, yes; passion rules my life. Love exists, but not with a big L."

The note read simply, *"Je regrette."*

Breathless (1960), directed by Jean-Luc Godard and starring Jean-Paul Belmondo, redefined international cinema. Belmondo's character, a casually ruthless car thief named Michel Poiccard, left the older generation gasping "*Quelle horreur!*" while the young clamored for more. Casual is the operative word. Belmondo's character was not a calculating criminal; he was an opportunist. Belmondo and Delon epitomized *sangfroid* (unfazed cold-bloodedness), unlike, say, Brando who projected humanistic heat even at his most alienated.

The *New Yorker* described the characterization as "icy animalism that apparently infects so many of our young and terrifies so many of the rest of us." Of the chemistry between *Breathless* co-stars Belmondo and Jean Seberg, the *New York Times* wrote, " . . . they come at you with terrifying power, he with the sinuousness of a serpent, she with the eerie force of a corrupted child." The actor became the center of a cultish following, known as *le belmondisme*.

A child of the bohemian milieu of St. Germain-des-Prés and Montparnasse, Belmondo was born in 1933 to a respected academic sculptor. Adored in France as "Bebel," Belmondo lacked intellectual pretensions, preferring instead straight-up action films which supported his image as

an existential punk. Much of his visual power rested in the expressive way he used his long, angular body, which could go from slack to electrifyingly alert in moments, giving him the aura of a predator in an entirely natural state of being. He mortified production crews by insisting on doing his own stunts, wrestling tigers and switching from a helicopter to a biplane in midair if the script demanded. Of an uncharacteristically introspective project, *Moderato Cantabile* (1960), written by Marguerite Duras, author of *The Lover*, Belmondo said, "It was very boring."

In a matter of four decades, French cinema distilled the convulsive social changes which preceded and followed the atomic age. While French leading men always seemed the least innocent of Latin Lovers, the New Wave established them as the steeliest. ❖

Belmondo co-starred with Delon in Borsalino *(1970), opposite, and with Jeanne Moreau in* Moderato Cantabile *(1960). Above, Jourdan was caught in the middle, hampered by old Gallic charm, yet yearning to be tough.*

ANTHONY QUINN
coyote laughter and
BLARNEY

Anthony Quinn's Mexican grandmother told him as a boy that he would one day grow up to be just like her film idols, Antonio Moreno and Ramon Novarro. But he did more than that; Quinn was to bring qualities to the screen which are uniquely his own. He is pure, swaggering sex with a five-day stubble, exuding a naturalistic masculinity which easily drew men in as trusted comrades, and made women seethe like water for chocolate. He radiates earthy maleness, more at home in hot sun and rawhide than moonlight and roses. In 1990, Federico Fellini said of him, "Anthony Quinn belongs to the species of actors I'm tempted to call 'landscape' actors, one who fills up a screen like a panorama."

In his youth, he had a middleweight boxer's body, and used his large frame expres-

As Hollywood's first leading man with unmistakably Azteca *Mexican features, Anthony Quinn was cast in roles of every ethnicity throughout his six-decade career.*

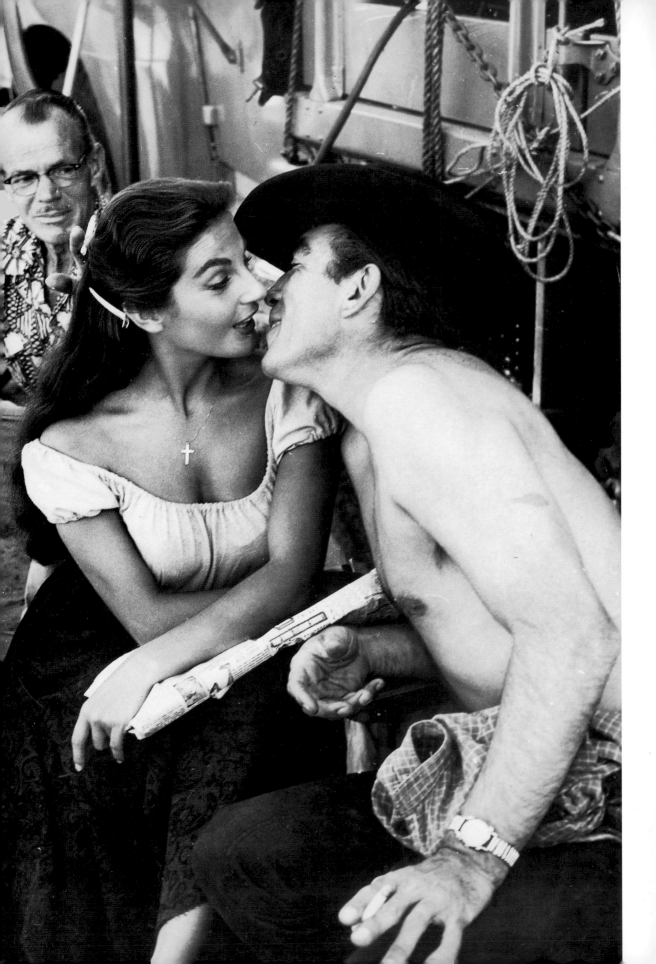

sively. His sexuality seemed primitive, like Brando's; in fact, Quinn played Stanley Kowalski in the national touring company of *A Streetcar Named Desire*, shortly after Brando had immortalized the role on Broadway. In 1950, the *New York Times* wrote, "If [Quinn] is less boorish than Marlon Brando of the original cast, he is only a little less boorish, and without sacrificing the animal exuberance, he may be a little more sensitive to the nuances of the character."

As a Latin Lover, Quinn emanated a rawness which made him a foe of feminists, but a magnet for women on- and off screen. Resisting him was as futile as fighting a force of nature. Even the normally frosty Barbara Stanwyck goes glassy-eyed in his brawny arms in *Blowing Wild* (1953). Perhaps against our own better judgement, we can't help but feel an animal rush when he roughly grasps Maureen O'Hara by her nape in *The Magnificent Matador* (1955). In the Dino De Laurentiis production of *Barabbas* (1962), a particularly brutish-looking Quinn wrestles Silvana Mangano into a kiss, at once both lion and lion-tamer.

Quinn seemed to gain erotic force as he aged. As a young actor, his slicked, dark hair and long, fringed eyelashes seemed incongruous to the toughness of his persona. In a crisp military uniform opposite Dorothy Lamour in *The Last Train From Madrid* (1937), or a pinstriped thug opposite Anna May Wong in *Dangerous to Know* (1938), his true heat and weight as an actor were yet to be unleashed. Fellini's black-and-white masterpiece, *La Strada* (1954) cast him as Zampano, a blustery circus strongman with a face and heart of stone. This transitional role was a defining one, positioning him as a callous antihero whose epiphany, and humanity, come too late. By the time he appeared in *Behold a Pale Horse* (1964), his temples were gray and his middle had thickened, but Quinn stayed sexy. Despite the signs of age, he shed his shirt on-screen and beckoned the voluptuous Daniela Rocca to his bed.

Unlike the more precious Latin Lovers of the silent era, or the suave lounge lizards of his own generation, Quinn would never be accused of being a fey *papi chulo*, or pretty boy. The Mexican-born actors who preceded Quinn were of Spanish lineage, and their skin tone and features reflected their European bloodlines. Quinn, on the other hand, was Hollywood's first leading man who was unmistakably *mestizo*, a rugged

Stubble and all, Quinn was always capable of stopping a passing señorita in her tracks. Here, the lissome Lita Milan, on the set of The Ride Back *(1957).*

mix of Native American and Irish heritages; he called his own bluntly sexy face, with its great, dark brows and wolfish smile, "*Azteca.*"

Quinn became Cecil B. De Mille's son-in-law when he married De Mille's daughter Katherine in October of 1937. It was a decision which created turmoil in both his professional and personal life. He had met the dark-haired beauty with the piercing eyes the previous year on the set of De Mille's film, *The Plainsman*, starring Gary Cooper and Jean Arthur. There was no courtship to speak of, according to Quinn, because Katherine was primarily interested in defying her adoptive father by "bringing home a hungry Mexican from the wrong side of town." They married when Quinn was twenty-two and Katherine was twenty-six years old, both actors under contract to Paramount. None of Quinn's relatives or friends were invited to attend the ceremony at All Saints Episcopal Church in Hollywood, which was curiously modest, considering the *dramatis personae*. That honeymoon night in Carmel, the marriage nearly ended when Katherine revealed that she was not a virgin; in fact, her past lovers had included Clark Gable and director Victor Fleming. The confrontation which followed forced her to flee by train to seek a quickie divorce in Reno. Quinn caught up with her en route, and they began to build a precarious life together.

Just as Quinn resented not being cast in leading roles, he grieved and raged at not being "first" with Katherine, a lifelong obsession which he chronicles in detail in his two autobiographies, *The Original Sin* (1972) and *One Man Tango* (1995). As these books reveal, Quinn then set out to pursue dual careers: to act, and to bed as many women as possible to compensate for his wife's past—clearly a case of the punishment far outstripping the crime.

He was born Antonio Rudolfo Oaxaca Quinn in Chihuahua, Mexico, in 1916, conceived in the midst of the Mexican Revolution "with nothing but snakes and lizards to help my mother bring me to life." The Quinn family lived in a boxcar during the smallpox epidemic of 1918, worked in the railroad yards setting ties where his father nearly lost a hand, and travelled the west as migrant workers picking walnuts, grapes, citrus, tomatoes and lettuce crops. Much of Quinn's rough-hewn appeal is born of the hardship and dignity of the Chicano experience which is

Quinn's rare moments of levity and tenderness are affecting. He's shown dancing with Rita Hayworth in Blood and Sand *(1941) and at right with Jody Lawrance in* Mask of the Avenger *(1951).*

deeply etched into the creases of his face. Militant on the subject of farmworkers' rights later in life, he formed a lifelong friendship with the late activist and strike organizer Cesar Chavez.

His first professional acting job came in 1936 when he was cast in the Los Angeles production of Mae West's play, *Clean Beds*. At the age of twenty, Quinn was unemployed and hungry, yet even this seemed to work to his advantage: his haggard appearance landed him his first walk-on film part in *Parole* (1936). Later that year, stranded in southern Texas and on his way to take a job on a fishing boat in Ensenada, he picked up a discarded Los Angeles newspaper. When his eye fell on a story about Cecil B. De Mille's difficulty in casting for *The Plainsman* (1937) because he couldn't find Native American actors who could speak Cheyenne, Quinn immediately hitchhiked back to California.

Arriving at the Paramount lot, he pretended that he couldn't speak English and proceeded to improvise a full gibberish script in pidgin Cheyenne. In fact, he even improvised an "authentic"

Cheyenne song, praying silently, "Make me an Indian, make me an Indian, right now for the next two hours."

The moral of this story: be careful what you wish for. Quinn's prayers were answered many times over, often to his dismay; for decades, he seemed confined to flamboyant ethnic roles. Throughout his career, his pan-racial face often dictated the content of his characters, ranging from Atilla the Hun (with taped eyelids) in *Atilla, Flagello di Dio* (1954), an early Dino De Laurentiis production, to Auda Abu Tayi (with false hook nose) in *Lawrence of Arabia* (1962) to Aristotle Onassis in *The Greek Tycoon* (1978). In the late thirties, he was frequently cast as Chinese, opposite beautiful Anna May Wong (*Daughter of Shanghai* (1937), *King of Chinatown* and *Island of Lost Men*, both 1939).

Yet his most enduring roles—in *La Strada*, as Paul Gauguin in *Lust for Life* (1956) opposite Kirk Douglas' Van Gogh, and, of course, as the delicious satyr Zorba (1964)—transcend their scripted nationalities to become the intimate companions of our imaginations. At his best, Quinn freqeuntly makes us believe that we have known his characters all our lives.

Always prolific, Quinn's career was a mixed bag in those years. He appeared in a third De Mille vehicle, *Union Pacific* (1939) and played Dorothy Lamour's jealous *novio* in *The Road to Singapore* (1940). He also appeared in *The Road to Morocco* in 1942. John Farrow directed him in *California* (1946) starring Barbara Stanwyck and Ray Milland, and, while on loan to Fox Studios, Quinn landed his first major role. In Rouben Mamoulian's remake of the Rudolph Valentino title, *Blood and Sand* (1941), he was cast as Manolo de Palma, a young matador who tries to steal the girl (played by Rita Hayworth) from

Juan Gallardo, played by Tyrone Power. As was usually the case, Quinn made Technicolor sparks fly both on- and offscreen. After bedding his fiery Latina co-star, her husband Orson Welles was quoted as saying, "If you're gonna have an affair, you could at least have f**ked Tyrone Power."

Seemingly trapped in a life where the leading man's crown was denied him—both with his work as well as with his women—Quinn told his emotionally dependent wife Katherine, "We're moving to New York—I'll never be anything but an Indian in this town." This decision seemed inevitable.

Quinn and his family finally moved to New York City in 1947, the year he became a U.S. citizen, where he was cast in the lead of *The Gentleman from Athens*. The play had the mixed blessing of opening within one week of Elia Kazan's original production of *A Streetcar Named Desire*, starring Marlon Brando. While *Streetcar* swiftly eclipsed *Gentleman* (the latter closed in one week), *Newsweek* described Quinn as "tough and ingratiating as a 'dese-and-dose' Quixote, tilting at windmills."

Nor did Quinn's performance go unnoticed by Kazan, who soon cast him as Stanley in the national touring company, a role he would play successfully for two years. Kazan later cast him in the prime part which landed his first Oscar, for Best Supporting Actor in the role of Eufemio Zapata opposite Marlon Brando's lead in *Viva Zapata!* (1952), scripted by John Steinbeck.

After stage roles including the part of Texas in Lynn Rigg's play *Borned in Texas* in

Quinn's marriage to Katherine De Mille brought both their share of grief.

1950, appearing in the road company of *Born Yesterday*, and in S.N. Behrman's *Let Me Hear the Melody* in 1951, Quinn seemed ready to return to filmmaking. A fourth child, Valentina, was born to the actor and his wife in 1952, and he embarked on a series of progressively more promising films, both in Italy and the United States. He made a dozen films in the fifties, including two of his most powerful, *La Strada* (1954) and *Lust for Life* (1956) and for which Quinn won his second Oscar for Best Supporting Actor.

Quinn met Iolanda Addolori, a Venice-born wardrobe assistant, in Rome on the set of *Barabbas* in 1961. Two of Quinn's major films were released the following year: David Lean's sweeping *Lawrence of Arabia* starring Peter O'Toole, and *Requiem for a Heavyweight*.

In spite of his marriage and his trans-Atlantic entanglement with Addolori, Quinn was linked with several women in the early 1960s, including British stage actress Margaret Leighton, his co-star of *Tchin-Tchin* on Broadway. In 1962, Iolanda became pregnant, and gave birth to Quinn's son Francesco in March, 1963, followed by Daniele Antonio the following year. In January, 1965, he and Katherine were divorced in Juarez, Mexico, after twenty-seven years of marriage, and soon afterward Quinn married Iolanda, already pregnant with their third son.

Just as he was building a family dynasty of children (thirteen at last count) and women (innumerable), by the mid-1960s Quinn's professional star was rising to its zenith as well. His title role in *Zorba the Greek*, opposite the callow Alan Bates as his half-Anglo, half-Greek "boss," proved the role of a lifetime. It was Quinn's performance, not the novel by the beloved Cretan Nikos Kazantzakis, which brought Zorba into the popular consciousness.

It was a tough act to follow. In the 1970s, Quinn's agent told him that, in the eyes of Hollywood, he had become "nothing but a fat Mexican." Recent work had paired him with top names such as James Coburn, Sophia Loren, Ingrid Bergman, Charles Bronson, Virna Lisi, Anna Magnani and Irene Pappas. Now close to sixty years old, choice parts were beginning to dry up.

In his personal life, events were anything but dry. Iolanda filed for divorce from Quinn in 1995 after learning of the birth of Patricia, the child Quinn conceived with his secretary Kathy

Benvin (whom he finally married in 1997). Iolanda lamented to *People* magazine that year, "I worked all my life to keep my husband in good shape. I gave him every day his vitamins, his pills."

Quinn continues to write, paint, sculpt, ride his beloved bicycle through the Italian countryside (a street in Cecchina di Roma, where he spends much of his time, is named for him), dote on his new, growing family in Rhode Island, and, of course, to act. In the modern-day parlance of author John Gray, Quinn is as Martian as they come, and the unapologetic purity of his machismo has invited uncounted visitations from Venus. Unshaven, uncouth, unrepentant and laughing all the way, he has breathed robust life into a rogue's gallery of characters who, while often less than noble, remind us of our own urgent humanity.❖

As much as he enjoys the fair sex, he is first and foremost one of the boys. Opposite, he's male-bonding with James Coburn in A High Wind in Jamaica *(1965). Above, he and Joan Perry appeared in* Bullets for O'Hara *in 1941.*

MARCELLO MASTROIANNI

la dolce VITA

In his defining role as a journalist in Federico Fellini's 1960 masterpiece, *La Dolce Vita*, Marcello Mastroianni looked as though he had seen it all. His worldly, hound-dog eyes could just as easily have been surveying the collapse of the Roman empire as the unraveling of contemporary Italian society. The experience didn't seem to fluster him—he was way beyond getting flustered. Instead, it made him tired. Regarding the woman rumored to have been his greatest love, actress Faye Dunaway, he commented, "I flirted with her out of boredom, but then her passion completely took me by surprise." Yet his boredom was as delicious to worldwide moviegoers as a serving of *zuppa anglaise*.

Like the French New Wave, epitomized by Alain Delon and Jean-Paul Belmondo,

Mastroianni—seemingly exhausted by the mere idea of sex—is a far cry from the passionate Latin Lover of yore. Yet women were more than willing to comfort and console him.

Mastroianni seemed to lack the energy to chase women, on-screen or off. And women found his seeming indifference irresistible. As an actor, he described himself as "the anti-Gable. He . . . and others like Gary Cooper, played strong, clean men, full of honesty and virtue . . . But I'm not a lover type, not in the conventional sense, anyway. There's no erotic charge in me." Of course, all his denials did not change the fact that women found the Italian hopelessly attractive. Perhaps his broken-hearted demeanor stirred heroic or maternal instincts; perhaps it worked because the broken-heartedness seemed real.

Mastroianni refused to wear shorts in public because of his "bird legs," and maintained "I'm not handsome, and I never have been," dismissing his comparatively short nose as "cute" and less than worthy of his classical Roman heritage. Far from the clotheshorse prototypes like Gilbert Roland or Cesar Romero, Mastroianni's appearance was invitingly rumpled. His drooping eyes and tousled hair suggested the aftermath of a hard *notte di amore*, and the prospect of slipping into his slender arms seemed as delicious as slipping into a warm, unmade bed.

> **His drooping eyes suggested the aftermath of a hard *notte di amore*, and the prospect seemed as delicious as slipping into a warm, unmade bed.**

Mastroianni's personal life mirrored the screen's bedroom farces. Rumors abounded among the international glitterati that at least a half-dozen of Europe's most beautiful women had keys to his country house in Lucca; his tolerant and long-suffering Roman wife Flora was not among them. In every significant relationship with a woman, Mastroianni would be revealed as the love-victim, each defeat only adding to his continental, chain-smoking weariness. He and Faye Dunaway met on the set of *A Place for Lovers* (1968). After two years of what she described as their "backstreet affair," Dunaway tired of being the lowest point of the triangle, and left Mastroianni for another actor. "I stopped

He introduced Italian existentialism into the Latin Lover's rich vocabulary. Rather than playing the voracious predator, his frequent role was the love-victim. Opposite, Mastroianni in Divorce Italian Style *(1961).*

taking Marcello's calls," she wrote in her autobiography, " . . . but Marcello wouldn't accept that our romance was over . . . and in the end it was he, not me, who was destroyed by our parting."

Soon ensconced with a consoling Catherine Deneuve, twenty years his junior, Mastroianni would later say of Dunaway, "She wasn't beautiful," dismissing her hands as "bony," her feet as "masculine," her knees as "sharp," and her nose as "squashed." However, friends murmured that she had been the love of his life, and that he grieved not filling her desire to bear his child.

Mastroianni and Deneuve did have a daughter, Chiara, but even that bond was insufficient; Deneuve walked out on him, too. He told the press, "When things ended with Catherine, something in me was broken

When Faye Dunaway stopped taking Mastroianni's calls he was crushed. Above, Dunaway and he appear in A Place for Lovers *(1968). Opposite, in* La Dolce Vita *(1960), Mastroianni appears with Anita Ekberg.*

forever." And when Flora finally followed suit and was spotted around Rome on the arm of a young consort, Mastroianni broke down and sobbed on Italian television.

Flora was the ultimate loss. She had been his support system for so many years. In 1950, seven years after escaping to Venice from a Nazi labor camp, a twenty-six-year-old Mastroianni had impulsively married his co-star in a local theater production, Flora Carabella. Bound by restrictive Italian civil law, Catholic commandment and personal inter-dependency (today the word is "dysfunctional"), the marriage persisted until 1972, despite his infidelities. The first marital crisis came with Mastroianni's appearance in *La Dolce Vita* a decade after they took their vows. After the premiere, he said, "The picture had a strange effect on me. It was like I was being administered a truth serum. Until then I was hiding my true self even from myself."

He left Flora briefly during the filming, but soon returned, and then began the process of bending the institution of marriage to its breaking point. The Italian press would later attack their native son, not because

of his adultery with Deneuve, or because the union had resulted in a child, but rather because he had left his wife. After his death, Flora described comforting Mastroianni "like a sister" throughout the subsequent years whenever one of his many liaisons ended in tears.

Mastroianni's persona was clearly the antithesis of his virile screen predecessors. He accepted his own weakness both in and out of character with a wistful sigh and a shrug, dismissing himself as "confused, immature, and cute—a man must not be cute," and claiming, "This Latin Lover thing is a burden. You go to bed with a girl and she expects a Latin Lover, something exceptional. It's enough sometimes to make you impotent!"

His persistent popularity in the United States in more than one hundred fifty films ranging from Fellini's *8½* (1963) and *City of Women* (1980) to *Divorce Italian Style* (1961), *Marriage Italian Style* (1964) and Robert Altman's *Ready to Wear* (1994), suggested that contrary to stereotype, it was Americans, especially American women, who were the true romantics. He was not the overt predator, but rather the passive, wounded prey and his vulnerability called upon the darkest erotic recesses of the female psyche. Ultimately, women found him seductive because of his failings, not merely in spite of them.

> **He was not the predator, but rather the passive, wounded prey and his vulnerability called upon the darkest erotic recesses of the female psyche.**

Mastroianni had well-publicized affairs with women ranging from Ursula Andress, Jacqueline Bisset and Romy Schneider (despite his stated preference for Italian women) to Nastassia Kinski, thirty-four years his junior (despite his stated preference for mature women such as Jeanne Moreau). He rebuffed Brigitte Bardot, his co-star in *A Very Private Affair* (1962) as "something to pin up on a wall." He even summoned Flora and daughter Barbara to the set in Geneva to protect him from the furious ankle-rubbing and back-arching of the screen's most overheated sex kit-

About American women, Mastroianni told Playboy, *"I've never seen so many unhappy, melancholy women. Poor darlings, they're so hungry for romance."*

ankle-rubbing and back-arching of the screen's most overheated sex kitten. Surpisingly, he quickly dismissed the surreally sexual Anita Ekberg, his co-star in *La Dolce Vita*, as "too much like a Martian." Yet the scene in *La Dolce Vita* with the pair splashing in Rome's Trevi Fountain would become unquestionably the most famous of Mastroianni's career.

While his dance card was truly international, he claimed ultimate loyalty to the women of Italy, able to identify their "homespun" body aroma, he said, even in the dark. The Italian media feasted upon his affair with the sumptuous Monica Vitti, but his eleven-time co-star Sophia Loren said of him, "He never fell in love with me. Our friendship is much too deep."

Like Belmondo, Mastroianni was truly a son of the new generation, a child of war, catastrophe, and the threat of total nuclear annihilation. His most enduring love relationship, apart from his marriage, was with director Federico Fellini, and through Fellini, Mastroianni became the alchemist's vessel for neorealism and expressionism in film. The modern world, through Mastroianni's eyes both as character and man, was a bleakly amusing place, where any exertion was a waste of time. This new moral universe, a modern flowering of the old southern Italian bit-

Whether behind the wheel of a sexy Italian sportscar (as in La Dolce Vita, *above), or in the arms of a ravishing Italian woman, Mastroianni always kept his cool.*

terness, contained absolutely no absolutes. It was a place where a long smoke and a cup of good espresso might be enough; if a woman shows up, so much the better, as long as she doesn't intend to stick around and make trouble.

Mastroianni's surname is a contraction of "*Maestro Giovanni*," a title applied to his cabinetmaker father in Fontana Liri, a small mountain town about fifty miles southeast of Rome. He once wrote, "The movies fit me, this work made of shadows. In my work, nothing is solid or firm . . . Movies don't last. They go bad like me." He died at the age of seventy-two of pancreatic cancer, with Deneuve and both daughters at his bedside. On the day following his death, the city of Rome draped the Trevi Fountain in black. *Addio, Maestro.*❖

TERRA NOVA
the MODERNS

The women's movement made the Latin Lover cower in his boots. Masculinity in general went under shrill attack, and conventional notions of manhood withered in the Gorgon-like gaze of Steinem, Friedan and their strident sisterhood.

Thus, by the mid-seventies, Hollywood's Latin Lover had never been more of an anachronism. There were two responses among Latin actors: to downplay their sexuality along with their ethnicity, or to go to the opposite extreme. In defiance of feminists who demanded "sensitivity" from men, many of cinema's most memorable contemporary characters are latter-day portrayals of the Latin Lover at his most chauvinistic.

As played by Sylvester Stallone and John Travolta in the seventies, the new Latin Lover

Like many Latin actors of his generation, Cuban-born Andy Garcia shuns the high life for home life, prizing familia *over fanfare. John Travolta, above, made dancing macho again.*

131

was the sort of guy who proudly displayed a large gold crucifix nestled in a luxuriant thatch of chest hair. While certainly not romantic in the tradition of Valentino, Novarro or Moreno, his on-screen character was permitted to exude an animal magnetism—or maybe Stallone and Travolta just couldn't help themselves.

The character was urban, working-class, and probably knew a thing or two about tuning an engine. He was not in touch with his inner child. He wasn't prone to sobbing (except perhaps during the Super Bowl). A direct retort to the male-bashing feminism of the time, he represented a return to a basic, almost archetypal concept of masculinity. Kicking off a high-testosterone backlash with their films, characters like Stallone's Rocky and Travolta's Tony Manero from *Saturday Night Fever* were multi-billion-dollar crowd-pleasers. Even these actors, however, ultimately moved into roles in which their masculinity is more complex, subtle, and therefore more contemporary. In the case of Latin stars such as Al Pacino, Andy Garcia, Raul Julia and Jimmy Smits, typically Latin roles (bad-guy cop, sexy bad-guy) were elevated beyond cliché by intelligence and restraint. Of the current crop, only Antonio Banderas carries the torch as pure matinee idol beefcake (or in his case, *biftek*).

As Michael, heir to the Corleone organized crime dynasty in Francis Ford Coppola's immortal *Godfather* trilogy (1972, 1974, 1990), the young Al Pacino possessed a face from a Pompeiian fresco. Just as silent-era actors suspended our disbelief by filling the screen with exaggerated action, Pacino riveted moviegoers with a kind of ancient stillness. Media at the time raved about his "wild street beauty." He portrayed his character's hardening into a contemporary Mafia don without any of the stereotypical "passionate," hair-pulling Latin flourishes. Instead, he commanded the audience's attention by reducing and refining his movements down to nearly telepathic suggestions. When he does speak, his voice is barely more than a whisper. His small body is coiled like a spring, waiting. When the spring finally releases its force, as in the scene where Michael slaps his WASP American wife, Kay, Pacino's intensity nearly shatters the screen.

Pacino personifies the new "Latin Lover" as perceived and played in the seventies, eighties and nineties. Only recently has Pacino been cast

Pacino starred as Michael Corleone in The Godfather *(1972). Here, Michael weds his ill-fated Sicilian bride, Apollonia, played by Simonetta Stefanelli.*

in the occasional romantic role, as in *Scent of a Woman* (1992). This is not to say that the *Godfather* films are without their sense of doomed romance. Apart from Michael Corleone's relationship with Kay, the poignant exchanges between Pacino and Marlon Brando as the patriarch Vito may only be called love scenes. Michael's heart is broken not by a woman, but by the romantic betrayal of *la famiglia*.

In the early and most significant years of his movie career, he portrayed dramatic characters who happened to exude an intense, southern Mediterranean sexual aura. Sex appeal for its own sake has never been his dominant offering, except in *Cruising* (1980), where, at a black-leather boys' club he poses the immortal question, "Hips or lips?"

Pacino has refused the gold lamé mantle of Hollywood. He has never maintained a West Coast address, preferring to live in New York to pursue his love of theater. He has never married, and has been consistently silent—even secretive—on the subject of his relationships with the actresses Jill Clayburgh, Marthe Keller, Tuesday Weld and Kathleen Quinlan. Unruffled by the suggestion that his personal life may be somehow troubled, he retorted in a 1984 *Rolling Stone* interview, "Stan Laurel was married six times, you gonna talk to him about his mother and father?" Pacino is a publicist's nightmare, eluding even the most persistent papparazzi, and spurning the television talk-show circuit even when releasing a new film.

> **Just as silent-era actors suspended our disbelief by filling the screen with exaggerated action, Pacino riveted moviegoers with stillness.**

Pacino's heir in this cinematic lineage is Andy Garcia, who played the role of Vincent Mancini, Michael Corleone's hot-headed nephew and illegitimate son of his assassinated brother, Sonny. The role earned Garcia a 1991 Academy Award nomination, and established him as a force to be reckoned with. Spurning easy pretty-boy roles, Garcia made an indelible impression in films including *Eight Million Ways To Die* (1986), *Stand and Deliver* (1987), *The Untouchables* (1987), *Black Rain*

(1989), *When a Man Loves a Woman* (1994) and *The Disappearance of Garcia Lorca (1997).*

Typically, Garcia keeps his dramatic movements small, stylized and concentrated. Like Pacino, he emanates a fire which gains momentum throughout the course of a given performance as the result of the actor's tight control. His classic Latin looks suggest heat, yet his demeanor is more ice than spice. His steeliness seems to be a mask topped by a vampire's widow's-peak—a mask which admirers fantasize about stripping away in a moment of abandon.

Garcia was born Andres Arturo Garcia Menendez in Havana, Cuba. His family arrived in Miami in 1961, when Andy was five years old. Since achieving stardom, Garcia has maintained a firewall of privacy regarding his personal life with his Cuban-born wife Marivi, whom he married in 1982, and their three daughters. He refuses to do nude scenes, much to the disappointment of some audiences, and has walked out on auditions when asked to remove his shirt. In spite of these restric-tions, Meg Ryan, his co-star in *When a Man Loves A Woman*, said, "When he's on-screen, he's very good at loving women. It's amazing the way he looks at them."

In 1994, Garcia warmed the hearts of Cubans and Cuban-Americans by documenting the career of bassist Cachao (Israel Lopez), the largely unher-alded father of the mambo who had been reduced to eking out a living on Miami's wedding-reception circuit. Garcia directed the 1993 feature-length film about Cachao's career, "*Como Su Ritmo No Hay Dos*" ("Like His Rhythm, There Is No Other"). Garcia asserts, "No one is more Cuban than me . . . My culture is the basis of my strength."

Just as Garcia is a smooth operator, Sylvester Stallone is rough around the edges. After he audi-tioned for actor-director Sal Mineo for a part in a stage version of *Fortune and Men's Eyes*, Mineo told Stallone "to forget acting as a career." Stallone

Andy Garcia's star on Hollywood's Walk of Fame validates what moviegoers knew from his first moment on-screen: Garcia radiates stellar Latin style.

worked in a zoo, cut fish in a fish market and sold umbrellas on New York City street corners on rainy days to survive.

There is a kind of grand pathos to Stallone. Born in a charity ward in Hell's Kitchen, the son of working-class Italian immigrant parents, his downturned eyes are filled with an old pain, suggesting dramatic potential which his steroid-crazed roles after Rocky Balboa have rarely addressed. In the first of the *Rocky* (1976) pictures, the boxer mumbles about being "just another bum from the neighborhood"—a rephrasing of Brando's "could'a been a contender" soliloquy from *On the Waterfront*. However flashy Stallone may become, we feel that he will always remember how it feels to be on the outside looking in.

Of the pre-Rocky years, he recalled to the *L.A. Free Press* in 1976, "I had given up acting completely. I lived over a delicatessen and I felt trapped there. I was too old to go back to school, and go back to school for what? So I started to write. I painted my windows black so I never knew what time it was, got an air conditioner so I never knew what the temperature was. I couldn't afford any furniture so I slept on a board and wrote by candlelight while standing at the refrigerator."

He wrote the first draft for *Rocky* in three days, and the sequel in just short of thirty hours. He later reminded the press, however, that he had attempted more than thirty screenplays prior to writing *Rocky*. Stallone was at his best as the Philly palooka, where his best-remembered line consisted of two words: "Yo, Adrian."

During the late seventies and eighties, Stallone became a caricature of himself, grotesquely exaggerating his super-developed body into that of a comic-book hero (Rambo, for instance), and delivering some of cinema's most tortured dialogue (*Rhinestone,* 1984, co-starring the equally exaggerated Dolly Parton, was perhaps the low point).

After leaving his first wife, Stallone surrounded himself with flashy beauties like Brigitte Nielsen, above. Raul Julia, opposite, embraces Kiss of the Spider Woman *(1985) co-stars Denise Dummont and Sonia Braga.*

High-profile women in Sly's life have included former wife, Amazon Brigitte Nielsen, socialite Cornelia Guest, actress Susan Anton, and supermodel Jennifer Flavin (whom he once jilted with an infamous Fedex-ed "Dear Jane" letter, and with whom he later had a child).

Stallone has been a fantasy figure throughout his career, although perhaps more a macho fantasy of adolescent boys than a love-object for women. However, in his most recent roles, the actor has surrendered his ultra-defined warrior's body, and played ordinary men who have never been on the business end of an AK47. This maturing of his image may open the possibility of roles in which viewers may finally come to know him not only as avenger, destroyer and annihilator, but also as lover.

Stallone's diametric opposite was Raul Julia, who starred with Sonia Braga and John Hurt in Hector Babenco's *The Kiss of the Spider Woman* (1985). His 1975 portrayal of Macheath (*Mack the Knife,* 1989), the seductive slasher in the Lincoln Center production of *Threepenny Opera*, was called "a sexual time bomb" by the *Village Voice*. The *Voice* wrote, "His sense of suppressed passion, in his heavily lidded eyes, his tense stance, his lascivious stare, in the erotic charisma of that scar, suggests a voracious sexual appetite—and what is more provocative than the mystery which suppressed passion evokes, what is more arousing than awaiting the explosion, knowing you'll be its object?"

Julia made every conversation into a seduction. His presence on stage and screen was predatory and knowing. He moved stealthily, using his body as strategically as a chess piece. Although his face was not classically proportioned—his eyes were far too large—he was mesmerizing. Much of his appeal was mental, projecting a wily intelligence behind his direct sensuality. Of the Puerto Rican-born actor, director Francis Ford Coppola said, "Raul's got swash and he's got buckle." Director Paul Mazursky analyzed his powers on-screen and stage by saying, "The thing you have to

realize about Raul Julia is that deep down, he thinks he's Errol Flynn."
Julia countered, "I don't think I'm Errol Flynn, but I've often wished I were."

Classically trained, his films choices ranged from Coppola's *One from the Heart* and Mazursky's *Tempest* (both 1982) to the role of Gomez in *The Addams Family* (1991) and *Addams Family Values* (1993) opposite the sleek Anjelica Huston as Morticia. Movie and theater critics occasionally skewered Julia for being too "broad" in his selection of roles. Julia considered this veiled criticism for not consistently playing self-consciously ethnic roles. He frequently reminded interviewers, "I didn't come to New York to be a stereotype." Julia, who was married to dancer-actress Merel Poloway with whom he had two sons, died in 1994.

From the very beginning, Travolta had the moves. As a boy, he studied the slick footwork of the Temptations and The Four Tops, bringing it all home to Brooklyn as Tony Manero in Saturday Night Fever *(1977).*

Television creates species of actors all its own, and John Travolta is one of these. Travolta personified the return of the Latin Lover as a low-life "greaser," starting with the role of Vinnie Barbarino, one of the "sweathogs" on the 1970s television series "Welcome Back, Kotter." Barbarino was the adorable hoodlum-next-door, a sanitized version of the "J.D."s (juvenile delinquents) portrayed in *West Side Story* and its many imitations. Travolta successfully jumped from the little screen to the big screen in his role as disco king Tony Manero in *Saturday Night Fever* (1977), filmed in the gritty Bay Ridge section of Brooklyn. Travolta persists as our eternal icon of dance fever in his black shirt and white polyester suit, hair laboriously coiffed into a prideful borough pouf, slick and utterly synthetic against the aural backdrop of keening Bee Gees vocals.

Dancing was critical to the role, as it was to Travolta's next iteration of the greaser-lover, Danny Zuko in the film version of *Grease* (1978). Barbarino, Manero or Zuko would have no use for the "soft" man of the seventies so eloquently described by Robert Bly; in fact, they'd kick his ass for being so soft.

In 1995, *GQ* wrote of Travolta's career, "He killed, once and for all, the culture of the sixties, crystallized the culture of the seventies, lit the flame under the culture of the eighties and ushered in a world in which we would forevermore be expected to know how to dance." No longer snake-hipped, he played a burly and imperfect angel in *Michael* (1996), still able to enchant a dance floor full of women with his small, laughing eyes and great moves. His dance scene with Uma Thurman in director Quentin Tarantino's *Pulp Fiction* (1994) is a cinematic moment as timeless as Marilyn Monroe's skirt billowing up over the subway grate in *The Seven-Year Itch* (1955).

Travolta's personal life has been remarkably void of scandal for a former teen heartthrob. Even at the peak of his boogie nights popularity, circumspect Travolta always seemed more interested in flying his private planes than high-profiling with the blonde of the moment. His youthful romance with the late actress Diana Hyland was followed by a long relationship with his lifetime friend, actress Marilu Henner. His marriage to Kelly Preston never makes headlines. Unlike the matrimonial pyrotechnics of a Stallone, Travolta is a family man whose stability is out of character for the stereotypical Latin Lover. Even though his star has risen to great heights twice in his career, he has not been blinded by its light.

It is difficult to imagine the long-running television series "L.A. Law" without Jimmy Smits as the young attorney Victor Sifuentes, a role he played for the show's first five years. Exuding a smoky, half-Puerto Rican, half-Surinamese sex appeal and dry sense of humor, Smits is laid-back on-screen, underscoring his high eye-candy quotient with a native Brooklynite's nonchalant toughness.

In 1987, he told the *Los Angeles Times*, "I'm flattered by the sex-symbol stuff, but it upsets me when it gets turned into a contest between me and the other guys in the cast. That 'who's the sexiest?' business is a crock that the media cooked up to sell magazines, so while I say thank you very much, I don't put much stock in it."

As Sifuentes, Smits liked to wear sneakers beneath his Armani suits whenever his feet were off-camera; the sneakers gave his character "bounciness," he said. Likewise, his sex appeal is youthful, modern and light on its feet. He is not puffy, heavy or grandiose, and this sense of accessibility adds to his attractiveness.

Of course, the magnetic lure of his six-foot frame (vertically-challenged "L.A. Law" co-star Michael Tucker joked, "Jimmy's entirely too tall to be a sex symbol"), dreamy eyes and cinnamon-hued skin speak for themselves. His memorable nude scene in Blake Edwards' *Switch* (1991) can only have enhanced the film's home-video success. Likewise, his nudity on television's "NYPD Blue" as Detective Bobby Simone is invariably the subject of morning-after water cooler chat in offices nationwide.

His parents moved the family from New York to Puerto Rico when Smits was ten years old. Although the relocation was

TV's sultriest cop, Jimmy Smits smirks off-camera with companion Wanda de Jesus. Smit's persona is understated, leaving the heavy breathing to fans.

initially traumatic, he told *New Woman* magazine in 1997, "It was the best thing that could have happened to me. It really cemented who I am. I am Puerto Rican." In June, 1996, Smits founded the National Hispanic Foundation for the Arts.

A divorced father of two, Smits played an icy drug czar in *Running Scared* (1986), a police officer drawn into the clutches of *santeria* practitioners in *The Believers* (1987), and the mustachioed General Tomas Arroyo in *Old Gringo* (1989) opposite Jane Fonda.

Unlike the reserved Smits, Malaga-born Antonio Banderas fulfills the fantasy of the Latin Lover at his most classic. He is at once leather and lace, merging uninhibited animal beauty with a teasing finesse. In her 1991 tour documentary *Truth or Dare*, a disbelieving Madonna screeched the news worldwide that he was unwilling to sleep with her—an opportunity which no self-respecting *mujeriego* (womanizer) would have turned down. Banderas has flashing dark eyes and a mane of unruly black curls. His lisping Castilian accent suggests a wet, almost swollen mouth, lips which seem too full and soft to hold a hard consonant. Like the classic Latin Lover, he sings—and rather well, as he demonstrated in his role as Che in *Evita* (1996). And he seems irresistibly dangerous. Boundaries don't contain him. He is untamed by delineations of matrimony, gender assignment, language or culture.

Banderas has often played gay men in films directed by Pedro Almodovar in his native Spain, yet he is a powerful conventional leading man. Simply, we believe in him as a lover—almost anyone's. He was utterly plausible as Tom Hanks' significant other in *Philadelphia* (1993) (in which Banderas' then-wife appeared as well), and the next year in *Desperado*, directed by Robert Rodriguez, the divine Salma Hayek seemed ready to melt into a cloud of steam once she was

Antonio Banderas is the last of the classical Latin Lovers. He is darkly sexy, a bit macho, a bit not. Neither female nor male fans can resist his charms.

astride him.

He seems unflappable by innuendo, dissolving boundaries like a pat of butter on hot toast. He was in an eight-year marriage and Melanie Griffith had reunited with her ex-husband, Don Johnson, when Banderas met her on the set of *Two Much* (1987). He swept Griffith into a heated romance that was a feast for the tabloids. The scandal resulted in marriage and baby daughter Estela in 1995.

Of his cross-gender, cross-cultural appeal, he has said, "I don't push the idea of the Latin Lover. I accept it. It doesn't worry me. I mean, it is only a question of time that I will be getting older and probably lose my hair."

He became one of Pedro Almodovar's regulars, starring in *Women on the Verge of a Nervous Breakdown* (1988) and *Tie Me Up! Tie Me Down!* (1990). He was equally sultry in *The Mambo Kings Play Songs of Love* (1992, his first U.S. film), *Interview with a Vampire* (1994) and he was one of the few Latino actors cast in the all-star film version of Isabel Allende's masterpiece, *House of the Spirits* (1994). In 1998, Banderas played the most fox-cunning swordsman of them all in *The Mark of Zorro*.

He has been studying English for several years, but shrugs off the suggestion that a language or accent could be a significant barrier to his international appeal. Banderas says simply, "As an actor, my country is the world." ❖

On hand for another Hollywood gala, Griffith and Banderas proved that a Latin Lover's romances are not always short-lived.

EPILOGUE

The sun has set over the long day of Hollywood's Latin Lover as Valentino, Boyer and their counterparts portrayed him. He was right at home in the smoky, *fin de siecle* cabarets of Paris and the suave night-clubs of the 1940s. He was a natural in the dusty heat of the border towns (especially if those were created on a Burbank back lot), but the modern world has stripped him of his power. The existence of the Latin Lover depended upon a last remaining bit of mystery.

The insidious spread of mainstream American monoculture has dissolved that mystery forever. McDonald's, Coca-Cola, CNN, Microsoft and other industrial superpowers have homogenized the world. The dark-eyed, foreign stranger who swept in seventy-five years ago swirling his cape and rolling his "R"s, is now wearing Adidas and talking on his cellular phone—just like Kevin Costner. Even Antonio Banderas is much less exotic than he would have been in the Golden Age of film. The Latin Lover never actually existed, but now he's even absent from the screen.

Still, the world will always love a lover. It always seems easier to love a lover who loves us first, and this has historically been the purpose served by Valentino's cinematic scions. If he is effusive, demonstrative, impassioned, we can more easily let ourselves be swept away. This extroverted attitude toward love runs contrary to white, middle-class America's style, and so the fevered kissing of hands, trailing kisses up to the elbow and finally to the lips (one cannot help but think of Gomez Addams, and of Pepe Le Pew and laugh) was left to the Latin Lover.

Perhaps he never really existed. Perhaps he is a necessary hallucination, a desperately wished-for respite from the drudgery of real life, real love, real marriage—as much a myth as any winged horse or feathered serpent. Perhaps. But, we still listen wistfully for his guitar below our balcony, his boot heels at our door.❖

ACKNOWLEDGMENTS

I offer my humblest thanks to the saints and *orishas* who made this work possible.

My heartfelt gratitude goes to my publisher, Paddy Calistro, of Angel City Press, for opening her door. And to Scott McAuley for his sage comments at the appropriate moments. Also, my thanks go to Peter Shamray and Ann Gray for setting this mysterious journey in motion.

My appreciation to graphic designers Sheryl Winter and Dave Matli. Many thanks to copy editor Jane Centofante for smoothing the way. Thanks, also, to Laura Gilbert and Wayne Ling for creating a beautifully printed book.

A very special thank-you to David Chierichetti for photos from his personal archive and for his remarkable knowledge. And thanks, too, to Luis Reyes for his photos and insights.

My gratitude to Lucie Arnaz and Desi Arnaz, Jr., Desilu, too, LLC and Elisabeth Edwards for generously supplying the fantastic, previously unpublished photographs of Desi Arnaz which appear in this book.

To the snickering coyote-spirit who guards the canyon beyond my door, thank you for snapping the spine of my self-seriousness again and again.

—Victoria Thomas, 1998

PHOTO CREDITS

Academy of Motion Picture Arts and Sciences, cover, 8, 30, 43, 44, 45, 51, 110, 120, 121, 123.
Archive Photo, 53, 77, 130, 133, 136, 142
Arnaz family (Desilu, too), 87, 88, 90-91, 96
Author's collection, vi, 10, 12, 14, 19, 21, 22, 24, 25, 28, 36, 37, 38-39, 40, 42, 52, 55, 56, 57, 59, 61, 67, 70-71, 72, 81, 83, 85, 97, 98, 101, 103, 111
David Chierichetti, v, 9, 10, 11, 12, 13, 14, 15, 16, 17, 22, 26, 27, 32, 33, 34-35, 46, 58, 62, 64, 65, 66, 69, 74, 75, 78-79, 100, 102, 105, 106, 107, 108, 109, 114-115, 118, 124, 125, 127, 128, 129, 138
Corbis-Bettmann, 76, 82, 99
Michael Jacobs, 137
Alfred Ortega, 131, 135, 141
Photofest, 63, 76, 112, 116
Luis Reyes, title page, 13, 47, 49, 50, 54, 84, 89, 92, 119, 141

RAP.

4-21-99

GAYLORD FG